Building a Province

Building a Province

60 ALBERTA LIVES

00662-4166

Brian Brennan

FIFTH
HOUSE
PUBLISHERS

Front cover photograph by Daryl Benson/Comstock
Cover and interior design by John Luckhurst/GDL

The publisher gratefully acknowledges the support of The Canada Council
for the Arts and the Department of Canadian Heritage.

THE CANADA COUNCIL   LE CONSEIL DES ARTS
FOR THE ARTS   DU CANADA
SINCE 1957   DEPUIS 1957

We acknowledge the financial support of the Government of Canada
through the Book Publishing Industry Development Program for our
publishing activities.

Printed in Canada.
99 00 01 02 03 / 5 4 3 2 1

Canadian Cataloguing in Publication Data

Brennan, Brian, 1943–
   Building a province

   ISBN 1-894004-53-1

   1. Alberta—Biography. I. Title.
FC3655.B73 2000   971.23'009'9   C00-910677-4
F1075.8.B73 2000

Fifth House Ltd.
A Fitzhenry & Whiteside Company
1511 – 1800 4 Street S.W.
Calgary, Alberta, Canada
T2S 2S5

1-800-387-9776

To Zelda

Contents

Introduction

Building a province takes many hands and many years. Alberta, as a relatively young province, is still a work in progress. Born in 1905, it has evolved through a growing period when its pioneering settlers and their children impatiently referred to it as "Next Year Country" to the point where a young premier named Peter Lougheed decided, in 1971, to call it "Now Country." Afterwards, perhaps realizing that Albertans are constantly sustained by the promise of better things to come—rising oil prices, good crops, fat cattle—Lougheed took to calling his province "Tomorrow Country."

In that respect, Lougheed was as much an optimist as Alberta's first premier, Alexander Rutherford, who declared in 1906 that "we are a hopeful people—we hope that our fond expectations will be realized."

"We have no pessimists in Alberta," said Rutherford. "A pessimist could not succeed."

Nor are there any pessimists in this book. All were destined to leave their mark, and Alberta gave them the opportunity. Whatever hare-brained theory I may have about these people representing the various people of Alberta, there is no doubt that they were typically Albertan in that they always looked to the future and saw their province as a place to grow.

Some were builders in the literal sense of constructing things out of bricks and mortar. Bill Pratt built the facilities for the 1988 Winter Olympics in Calgary. Fred C. Mannix built highways, pipelines, and airports. And Jean Hoare built a restaurant in Claresholm that was the finest for miles around.

Others were builders of community. Henry Wise Wood organized a group of farmers into a powerful political movement. Betty Mitchell formed a network of community theatres throughout southern Alberta. Eric Harvie created a museum for Calgary that would house the finest collection of western artifacts anywhere. Catherine Barclay helped establish the basis for a national network of youth hostels. "Badger" Bob Johnson built a group of mediocre hockey talents into a Stanley Cup-winning National Hockey League team. And Morris Shumiatcher built a white cowboy hat into an internationally recognized symbol of Calgary.

Many of the stories, as you would expect from a province not yet one century old, are about people who came to Alberta from other places and, in some manner, helped define their new home. They brought their energies and their talents, and they built a province that still runs on energy—and I don't mean the kind that comes gushing out of the ground. Ontario operates in an atmosphere of smug satisfaction, British Columbia is stereotypically (and perhaps unfairly) consigned to mellow oblivion, and Alberta is the young province that rolls up its sleeves, works hard, asks no one for help, and gets the job done.

Alberta can also be seen as a welcoming haven for some of the rogues, the scoundrels, and the misfits of this world, and a few of their stories are included here as well. Without hoaxers such as Long Lance and George DuPre, and mavericks such as Jimmy "the Con" Carleton and Webster Macdonald Sr., Alberta would have to be painted in various shades of grey. "Here, nobody bothers us—we are left to live out our lives in whichever way suits us best," said Sarah Rampa, the wife of an impostor named T. Lobsang Rampa, an English ad man turned Tibetan mystic who found sanctuary in Alberta after being denounced as a charlatan in England.

A few of the stories are about people who started out in Alberta and made their contributions elsewhere. I liken these to the stories of such Irish writers as James Joyce, Bernard Shaw, Oscar Wilde, Samuel Beckett, Sean O'Casey, and Edna O'Brien, who made their major contributions while living in exile yet always remained Irish through and through. Wilf Carter achieved his greatest country music glory on the stages of Nashville and New York, but he remained an Albertan. The same holds true for Roloff Beny, who never failed to tell his high-society European friends that he came from Medicine Hat and that his work as a photographer was defined by his prairie upbringing.

Most of these people I have met only posthumously, through my work as a journalist in Calgary and as a researcher of Alberta history. They have taught me how to be an Albertan. I look over my shoulder as I write their stories, and I can see my room filling up with ghosts—both the ghosts of the people themselves, and the ghosts of certain editors who have supported me in my lifelong quest, born of my Irish upbringing, to make the storytelling as important as the subject matter.

"Make the words sing," says Reg Vickers, an editor for whom I spent a rewarding five years writing stories for the *Calgary Herald's* old *Sunday* magazine.

Reg died in May 1994, and that left me lamenting the loss of a rare newspaperman who cared as much about literary style as he did about informational content. A story didn't become a story in Reg's mind until it was endowed with the felicities of fine writing. Otherwise it was nothing more than data.

Ken Hull, who died in September 1999, subscribed to the same journalistic philosophy. During the years he wrote business and sports stories for the *Calgary Herald*, Ken cultivated the art of storytelling just for the sake of storytelling. It didn't matter what the subject was. The art, for Ken, was in the way the words came together.

"Just write stories," he said in October 1992, when I asked him how he expected me to approach the task of writing a daily column of feature obituaries and social history that he had just assigned to me. It didn't matter to Ken whether the subjects were famous or obscure, rich or poor, scintillating or boring. It didn't even matter to him that the people might have died a long time ago. He asked only that I try to give readers what people in the newspaper business refer to as a good read.

I don't know whether I ever really measured up to his expectations. Ken never told me. Newspaper editors of my generation rarely dispensed compliments. They only commented on your stories when you screwed up.

But I do know Ken always ensured there was a generous amount of space in the paper for my words. And I know he told his copyeditors that a story about a life well lived—even a life devoid of large triumphs—could sometimes be more compelling than a story about a convenience store robbery or the building of a new convention centre. Because of Ken's encouragement, I could invariably find a good reason for reminding readers that McMahon Stadium in Calgary was named after a couple of oilmen named McMahon, or that Johnny Bright Sports Park in Edmonton was named after a famous football player. I even found an excuse once to write about Robbie Burns, to mark the two hundredth anniversary of the Scottish poet's death.

The voice of Jack Peach also rings in my ears. Jack was a prolific Calgary social historian who scanned the obituary pages for me every day, looking for significant names from the past that might not mean much to someone with my shorter memory. "Make sure you mention Pearl Borgal," he says.

Who was Pearl Borgal? If it hadn't been for Jack, I might never have known. She was a Lethbridge sportswoman of incredible versatility who won Alberta provincial championships during the 1920s and '30s in basketball, swimming, golf, speed skating, and grass hockey. She coached swimming and riding, organized all-female rodeos, then went on to added glory in the 1950s as Canada's first female sportscaster at CKXL Radio in Calgary.

Jack phoned me regularly with tips for my column. When he died in November 1993 at age eighty, I lost an important link with Alberta's past. I could still look up people in the files, but I couldn't talk to the one person in town who seemed to have a personal connection with everyone who had left a mark on this province during the previous seventy-five years.

I have many people to thank for supporting me in this work. Along with Reg Vickers and Ken Hull, I wish to thank the other *Calgary Herald* editors, former and current, who allowed me to write with great freedom and scope, handled my words with care, and put most of them in the paper. And I want to thank all the historians—the professionals who write in journals and the amateurs with long and reliable memories—who phoned, wrote, or sent e-mails of encouragement to me, gently corrected my errors of fact, and urged me to continue doing this work.

Lastly, I want to thank Charlene Dobmeier, my supportive editor at Fifth House, who showed me how a disparate selection of short biographies—each conforming in length to the span of attention that a listener might give to an oral narrator—could be fashioned into a larger, thematically unified whole. I used to think my stories were like products of the Irish verbal tradition, meant only to last as long as they lived in the ear of the listener. Now, thanks to Charlene, I have discovered that some of them may deserve to live longer than a single sunrise.

Brian Brennan
Calgary, May 2000

Dedication – Bill Gold

Journalist

1936–2000

Bill Gold was associate editor of the *Calgary Herald* when I came to work at the paper in the spring of 1974. He struck me immediately as a journalist I could admire and try to emulate, a thinker and a writer who saw newspapering as a business with a conscience and a higher purpose. Gold continued to impress me until the day he left the paper, 26 July 1996. Multiple sclerosis had prematurely ended his career at age fifty-nine.

We were not particularly close. When I joined the paper, Gold was in senior management, responsible for the *Herald's* editorial and opinion pages. I was a reporter, then responsible for gathering police and court news.

But because he was an editor who wrote a column, I could get a strong sense of who Gold was and what he stood for as a journalist. He carried the torch for integrity, truth, taste, decency, and all the other good qualities that—I liked to believe—the *Herald's* readers would want their newspaper to epitomize.

Readers learned from his columns that Gold believed the main business of the *Herald*, no more no less, was to faithfully mirror the imperfect world in which it existed.

That meant telling every side of the story without giving preferential treatment to those who—because they bought advertising space—considered themselves to be the *Herald's* friends. A good newspaper did not have any friends, said Gold. The best journalism was practised selflessly in the public interest, not for the benefit of those who cared more about private profit than public debate.

The best journalism always saved its best shots for the government, said Gold. Responding to a group of land developers who accused the *Herald* of persecuting them, he said: "We really can't afford the luxury of singling out some special group—other than politicians—to loathe with some special passion."

His refusal to play ball with advertisers occasionally landed Gold in trouble with his eastern bosses, the corporate owners of the *Herald*. They believed the newspaper's main business was to make money. Gold believed otherwise. He flatly refused to sacrifice journalism at the altar of advertising revenues.

On one memorable occasion, after being appointed editor in chief in 1976, Gold told local movie theatre managers he would happily risk losing all of their advertisements rather than bow to their demands to stop running capsule critiques in the *Herald's* weekly movie guide. "Double jeopardy," they protested. "Don't mess with the press," replied Gold, or in words to that effect. The movie people capitulated and dropped their threat to pull their advertisements.

Gold worked in a few nonwriting management positions at various points during his lengthy, on-again off-again stint with the *Herald*, which started in 1956 when he was nineteen. But he always came back to writing.

The *Herald* was happy to have him back. It was even happy to have him back in 1987, after he had spent 14 months working as editorial director for the competition, the *Calgary Sun*. Demonstrating a rare lapse in judgment, Gold had jumped into the arms of the tabloid competitor after a disagreement with the *Herald* publisher at the time, Pat O'Callaghan.

Gold and O'Callaghan were uneasy bedfellows, two larger-than-life newspaper personalities with egos to match. Gold described their testy relationship in one column: "Do Pat and I disagree on some things? You bet we do. Show me a paper where the editor and publisher don't pummel one another at regular intervals, and you've shown me one that's sound asleep."

This "pummelling" precipitated a temporary separation when Gold jumped to the *Sun*, but the divorce papers were never filed. Gold and O'Callaghan settled their differences, and Gold returned to enriching the *Herald* with what O'Callaghan called "top-quality journalism from a sensitive and informed writer whose craftsmanship has always been admired by his peers."

Gold had cultivated his craftsmanship without benefit of a high school diploma or formal equivalent. He was autodidactic and proud of it. "Surely the last editor of a major paper in Canada to own no certificates of school completion beyond Grade eight," he said. Born in Saskatoon, he had left home at age fifteen and worked in construction and dairy farming before joining the *Ottawa Journal* as a junior reporter the following year. Nine years later he was writing editorials for the *Calgary Herald.*

He spent most of his working life at the *Herald.* When he retired on disability leave in 1996, he wrote a farewell column characteristic of his very best work. With grace, intelligence, economy of words, and an utter lack of emotion, Gold described his newspaper life as having been one of "working with good people, and being read by good readers."

"For me, goodbyes are for gravesides," he wrote. "And so are most of the reminiscences that these occasions so often evoke."

None of his colleagues wanted to say goodbye to him then, and it's hard to say goodbye now. His voice was stilled all too soon. What would he have said about the Canadian Alliance, the legacy of "Rocket" Richard, the airlines merger, Bill 11, or the Alberta "senators-in-waiting"? One misses his clear thinking and fine writing. In the best tradition of Walter Lippmann, the famous American columnist who showed him the way, Gold would have beamed his searchlight onto each issue and brought it out of the darkness into vision.

Gold died of liver cancer in May 2000, at age 63. Shortly before his death, a group of friends started a scholarship fund in his name to be given to the school of his choice. Gold chose Calgary's Mount Royal College. He had never gone to an institution of higher learning, but at the end of the day he was proud to have his name associated with one.

Leonard Gaetz

Homesteader and founder of Red Deer

1841–1907

For the buffalo hunters who migrated between the eastern plains and the western foothills, and for the fur traders who followed them in the late eighteenth century, the place that was to become Red Deer was nothing more than a stop along the way—a sheltered river valley where they could camp for the night before moving on. But for Leonard Gaetz and the other white settlers who arrived in the area during the 1880s, it was an idyllic parkland location, where, said Gaetz, "I would rather take my chances in the industry of farming than in any spot on Earth either south or north of the forty-ninth parallel."

Gaetz, who called himself a "pilgrim," moved to the farming country of central Alberta for a number of reasons: "poor health, poverty, and a desire to keep my family around me." Born in 1841 in Musquodoboit Harbour, Nova Scotia, he had become a Methodist minister at age nineteen and served some of the largest congregations in Canada. In 1883 he suffered a nervous breakdown and had to find a new way of life to support his growing family. With his pregnant wife, Caroline, and their ten children, plus four horses, sixteen head of cattle, and provisions to last a year, Gaetz left his farm home in Hamilton, Ontario, in April 1884 and moved west as far as the railway would take him.

After a few weeks in Calgary, where his family stayed in two shacks loaned to them by generous Calgarians ("the kindest of the dwellers of these western plains"), Gaetz and his three oldest sons headed north to look for a homestead. They found their spot on an abandoned horse ranch three miles downstream from where the north-south wagon trail between Edmonton and Calgary crossed the Red Deer River. At the crossing itself, there was a small settlement consisting of a handful of homes and a trading post owned by a man named King.

Gaetz and his three sons built a large log house on a hill near the river. His wife, Caroline, and the rest of the children joined them the following month. They planted oats, barley, wheat, and potatoes for their own use, and turnips and hay for the livestock. The crops, aided by an abundance of summer rain, did well.

In August 1884 Gaetz acquired the trading post from King and placed his eighteen-year-old son Ray in charge. Ray advertised his wares in the *Calgary Herald* and learned to speak Cree so that he might trade with the Natives.

During the Riel Rebellion in April 1885, Gaetz fled with his family to Fort Calgary for protection. During their absence, they suffered losses for which the federal War Claims Commission eventually compensated them.

Gaetz proved to be an accomplished farmer, and the family's crops did well throughout the 1880s. He was also a tireless booster for the district. He wrote a number of promotional articles for the *Calgary Herald* and travelled to Ottawa, where he testified on the agricultural potential of the region before the Select Standing Committee on Agriculture and Colonization. The federal government circulated his testimony, subsequently printed as a pamphlet entitled *Report of Six Years' Experience of a Farmer in the Red Deer District*, as a fact sheet for potential settlers.

Gaetz told the government committee that settlers would flock to the area when a railway was put through. The government responded by charting the Calgary and Edmonton Railroad Company in early 1890. Gaetz offered the company a half interest in his twelve-hundred-acre farm if the railway would cross the river on his property. The company readily accepted the offer. In November 1890 a new townsite was surveyed on the Gaetz farmland, and the future city of Red Deer was born. On 23 November, when the first passenger train travelled from Red Deer to Calgary, Gaetz, his wife, and one of their daughters were among the passengers on board.

A flurry of construction activity followed the arrival of the railway in Red Deer. In March 1891 the *Calgary Herald* reported the building of five new stores—one belonging to Ray Gaetz—plus a hotel and several new homes. The finest of these was the two-storey Gaetz home, built at a cost of nearly $3,000. The house remained standing until the 1950s, when it was demolished to make way for a gas station and shopping plaza.

The Gaetzes were truly the first family of Red Deer, prominent in all aspects of the community's life. Leonard Gaetz was chairman of the first school board, while Ray was secretary. Ray was also president of the first board of trade, and he became the first mayor when Red Deer was incorporated as a town in 1901.

Leonard was in great demand as a public speaker. He was offered a Senate appointment that he declined—it went instead to James Lougheed of Calgary—and in 1893 he installed the Alberta grain exhibit at the Chicago World's Fair.

In 1895 he returned to the ministry, accepting a pastorate in Brandon, Manitoba. But six years later he came back to Red Deer and built a small retirement home for his wife, who was then in failing health. He added a library annex where he could work and meet with business associates without disturbing Caroline. Today that library is part of the Heritage Square section of Red Deer's Rotary Recreation Park.

Caroline Gaetz died in December 1906. Leonard died the following June, on the eve of his sixty-sixth birthday.

The Gaetz name has been synonymous with Red Deer ever since. "No other name has been so long, so continuously, and so honourably associated with Red Deer," declared the city's board of trade president at a ceremony honouring Ray Gaetz in 1934. The Gaetz name, at that point, graced a main thoroughfare, a lake, a park, a pharmacy-cum-bookstore, and a church. The list later expanded to include an elementary school, design group, car dealership, and tile contractor. The Gaetz clan had earned the undisputed right to call Red Deer "our town."

For many drivers travelling Highway 2 between Edmonton and Calgary, Red Deer is still just a stop along the way: a place for a coffee break and a gas fill-up. But for those who decide to stay a while, it offers an opportunity not just to see the town that Gaetz built, but also to commune with the great man himself. Visitors will find a bronze statue of the bearded Leonard Gaetz seated on a bench outside a coffee house, at the corner of Gaetz Avenue and Ross Street.

11

Sir James Lougheed

Lawyer, entrepreneur, and senator

1854–1925

Two buildings in Calgary have stood as monuments to James Lougheed, the contractor's son from Toronto who rose to become early Calgary's leading citizen and the grandfather of a future premier.

One structure is the big sandstone mansion Lougheed built as his home. From the late 1990s onward, it was being restored to its former glory as a magnificent example of late Victorian home building in the colonies. The other Lougheed development, located in the heart of Calgary's business district, was one of the last Canadian examples of a turn-of-the-century commercial building with a theatre contained within. It was scheduled for demolition in the spring of 2000, despite the efforts of a valiant group of heritage preservationists.

Both buildings have stood as visible reminders of how Lougheed left his mark on the city. He forged a connection with Calgary when it was little more than a motley collection of squatters' tents and shacks on the banks of the Bow and Elbow Rivers.

Lougheed's future, as he envisaged it as a young man, was wherever Canada's first transcontinental railway took him. He grew up in the impoverished Cabbagetown section of Toronto and was all set to follow his father into the building trade when a lawyer named Samuel Blake, who taught him at Sunday school, suggested he raise his sights higher: "Boy, you have too good a head to be a carpenter," Blake told him. "Why don't you take up the law?"

Lougheed joined a Toronto law firm as a student in 1877. He became active in Conservative politics at the same time and worked on the campaign that returned Sir John A. Macdonald to power in 1878. Macdonald had been forced to resign in 1874, in the wake of a scandal involving campaign contributions given to him and his Conservative colleagues by the promoters of the Pacific railway.

In 1882 Lougheed moved to Winnipeg, where he set up business as a lawyer. The next year he followed the Canadian Pacific Railway construction crews to Medicine Hat. Armed with a letter of introduction to the railway company's chief engineer, he persuaded a trainload of railway executives, including Sir William Van Horne, to take him on as a company lawyer in Calgary. Lougheed reached the tiny hamlet of Fort Calgary just before the railway, in August 1883. He was among the small group of welcoming enthusiasts who waved to the first locomotive as it steamed in over the East Calgary Bridge.

From the outset, Lougheed saw Calgary as the place where he could make his name and fortune. He believed that this community of squatters and Natives, barely a village yet, much less a town, would become the business hub of the entire Northwest, and that he would tap into its economic growth to make a comfortable living for himself. He bought the only log cabin in town, rented out the back half, announced to all and sundry that he was in business as a lawyer and solicitor, and started buying up lots at $300 apiece.

His choice of location seemed curious at first. The lots were situated more than a mile west of the townsite, and most people believed the town would expand to the east. Did Lougheed, because of his position with the railway corporation, have access to privileged information? No one has ever said. Lougheed continued to add to his holdings, acquiring some thirty lots in all.

When the railway established its main station building just one block from his property, Lougheed's fortune and future were assured. The land he had bought on speculation ringed the heart of the new town.

In September 1884 Lougheed solidified his links with the West when he became a member of the frontier aristocracy through marriage. His bride was Isabella Hardisty, known to friends and family as Belle, from Fort Victoria in the Northwest Territories. Her father, William Hardisty, was a Hudson's Bay Company factor in the Mackenzie River valley and the richest man in the Northwest Territories. Her mother, Mary Allen, was the English-speaking daughter of a Métis mother and her white husband. Her uncle was Donald A. Smith, the chief financial backer of the CPR and the future Lord Strathcona. Lougheed met Smith for the first time in 1885 and said afterwards that he "had quite a chat with the worthy driver of the last CPR spike."

Belle's Métis heritage was never an issue during the early years of her marriage to Lougheed. Mixed-blood marriages were common in the frontier society at that time. However, as Lougheed's position grew, he had to face taunts about his "Indian" wife. If it bothered him, it never showed. Belle was the first lady of the district, thanks to his business and political success.

His political fortunes increased dramatically in 1889, when Belle's uncle, Senator Richard Hardisty, was killed in a wagon accident. Calgary residents petitioned John A. Macdonald for another senator and nominated Lougheed as a "gentleman of culture, ability, and position, with a thorough knowledge of and faith in Alberta." The prime minister, remembering Lougheed's support in his 1878 campaign, accepted the nomination and appointed him to the Senate. Lougheed was just thirty-five.

Lougheed celebrated his heightened status in the community by building a palatial new home for himself and Belle. Located just beyond the confines of the growing city, it occupied the equivalent of an entire city block. Calgarians called it "the big house" and soon it became the centre of the city's social life. The Lougheeds named it "Beaulieu" for Belle's Métis ancestors.

Two British princes who later became kings, Edward VIII and George VI, occupied the mansion's bedrooms as guests. The Duchess of Connaught, whose husband was a son of Queen Victoria and the governor-general of Canada, described the house in her diary as "very comfortable." She was particularly impressed by the terraced gardens.

With business and political interests occupying more of his time, Lougheed invited a young lawyer from New Brunswick, Richard B. Bennett, to join his law firm as junior partner. The senator and the future prime minister of Canada worked together for more than two decades until they argued over Lougheed's attempt to dissolve the partnership without Bennett's agreement. In the early twentieth century, the firm of Lougheed and Bennett was one of the largest and most respected in the West.

The law firm's success allowed Lougheed to pursue his interest in real estate, and his buildings soon dominated the Calgary skyline. He named four of them, the Clarence Block, Edgar Block, Norman Block, and Douglas Block, after his sons. During the First World

War, and for several years afterwards, Lougheed was assessed fully half the property taxes in the entire city of Calgary.

In 1912, during the height of Calgary's first construction boom, he unveiled his most notable commercial building project. The six-storey Lougheed Building contained a fifteen-hundred-seat theatre, the Sherman Grand, hailed by the English actor Forbes Robertson as "one of the finest and most commodious theatres in all of western Canada."

Robertson was the guest performer in the Sherman Grand's opening production, a melodrama entitled *The Passing of the Third Floor Back*. During the decades following, the theatre served as a performance venue for a host of international touring stars, including Sarah Bernhardt, Lillie Langtry, George Arliss, and Dame Nellie Melba. It also featured a few rising hopefuls, including, in the fall of 1912, Fred Astaire and his sister Adele. Astaire was only twelve at the time. Considered too young to headline on Broadway, he toured Canada instead. The *Calgary Herald* characterized the brother-sister act as "two clever youngsters who are compelled to stay indoors on a rainy day."

The Sherman Grand was named after Lougheed's building partner, William B. Sherman, a flamboyant showman from Ohio who also built such Calgary landmarks of the period as the Sherman Opera House and the Sherman Rink, a combination roller rink, dancehall, and multi-purpose auditorium. Lougheed was happy to let his extroverted partner act as the front man while he remained behind the scenes. It would have been entirely inappropriate for a respected senator—especially one with a strict Methodist upbringing that denied such pleasures as playing cards, dancing, and going to the races—to be seen hanging out with common showbiz types.

But that's not to say that Lougheed distanced himself entirely from the Sherman Grand. He and Belle loved the theatre. As one of the Sherman Grand's managers said in the 1920s, "Whenever in the city, one of his greatest delights was to be present at one of our performances."

Lougheed spent more time in Ottawa than he did in Calgary after his Senate appointment. He served as Conservative leader in the Senate from 1906 to 1921, and served as acting minister of the militia during the First World War. For his efforts, the king knighted him in June 1916; he was the first and only Albertan to be so honoured. His partner Bennett later received a peerage, but he had to leave the country to accept it.

Lougheed died in 1925 at age seventy-one, after an attack of pneumonia and bronchitis. He left an estate worth more than $1.5 million, most of it in property holdings. The *Calgary Herald* obituary described him as a "noted western statesman."

The Lougheed mansion remained in the family until 1935, when it was seized for tax arrears and sold. The Red Cross acquired it in the late 1940s, and many Calgarians, including the future premier Peter Lougheed, grandson of Sir James, gave blood in the elegant surroundings.

In 1979 the Red Cross traded the house and part of the original grounds to the provincial government in exchange for a new administration building. A caretaker was hired to protect the mansion from vandals while the government determined its future as a possible historic resource.

During the 1990s the city of Calgary acquired the rest of the grounds—which had been sold to an apartment developer in 1950—and earmarked the entire property for redevelopment as a civic park. The park project, known as Beaulieu Gardens, was completed in 1998. The next phase in the project was to refurbish the old sandstone mansion itself, and that work was continuing through the beginning of 2000. Still in good shape, the house is opened up regularly for fund-raising Victoria teas, movie shoots, and wedding photographs.

As for the other notable component of the Lougheed building legacy, it survived both as a commercial building and as a theatre until the 1990s, when the owners decided that a six-storey office block was no longer a viable economic structure in a prime downtown location surrounded by high-rise office towers. An appeal to the province to have it designated as a historic resource fell on deaf ears. "Many of its heritage characteristics have been obscured," said a city official. In early 2000 this fabled historic building, which bears one of Alberta's best-known names, sat under the wrecker's ball, awaiting demolition.

Bob Edwards
Newspaper publisher
1859–1922

Bob Edwards was Calgary's first media celebrity, a genuine pre-television superstar who put the frontier town on the North American map long before cowboy showman Guy Weadick launched the Calgary Stampede or Mayor Don Mackay presented the first white cowboy hat to a visiting dignitary. "Calgary," said a New York politician in the early 1900s, "is, I believe, a place in Canada where the *Eye Opener* comes from."

The *Eye Opener* was Edwards's "newspaper," a satirical publication that broke all the accepted rules of journalism by running gossip and satirical commentary instead of news. Yet it enjoyed the largest circulation (thirty-five thousand) of any newspaper published west of Winnipeg.

Edwards started the paper in 1902, eight years after arriving in Canada. Born in Edinburgh, he was educated at a private school and Glasgow University and continued his studies in Berlin, Paris, and Rome. By the time he was thirty, he had seen most of Europe and had edited a gossipy newspaper, the *Traveller*, for the entertainment of wealthy tourists to the Riviera. Edwards enjoyed Nice and Monte Carlo at first, but his experiences there eventually showed him the shallowness of high society. "Gorgeous hats on empty heads made him realize that much of society is founded on false values and humbug," wrote his biographer, Grant MacEwan.

In 1892 Edwards immigrated to the United States "to ranch and be away from relations." He worked on a farm in Iowa, then headed north to Canada, hoping to become a homesteader. His total possessions at the time consisted of his clothing, thirty-five dollars in cash, and a book of Robert Burns's poems.

Edwards never became a homesteader. Instead, he went to Wetaskiwin, took a room at the Walker House Hotel, and, with financial help from the hotel owner, started a weekly newspaper.

Edwards came from a respectable Scottish publishing family named Chambers, so he did have ink in his veins. But there was nothing respectable about his paper. The booze-loving Edwards wanted to call it the *Wetaskiwin Bottling Works*, but friends persuaded him that *Wetaskiwin Free Lance* would sell more copies.

The paper didn't do well. Wetaskiwin, with its population of "287 souls plus three total abstainers," simply couldn't support it. After a brief stint with a second paper, which he wanted to name the *Strathcolic*, Edwards moved to High River in 1902 to launch his famous *Eye Opener*. He chose the name, he said enigmatically, "because few people will resist taking it."

The itinerant *Eye Opener* lasted two years in High River before moving to Calgary, where Edwards finally found a congenial setting for his alcohol-fuelled satire. Calgary, he noted approvingly, was "picturesquely situated so as to be within easy reach of the brewery, with streets revolving in eccentric orbits around a couple of dozen large bars."

While he often promoted the virtues of boozing in his columns ("a drink in the hand is worth two in the bottle"), it was characteristic of the unpredictable Edwards that when Alberta held a Prohibition vote in 1915, he supported the anti-liquor faction. "We've been there," he explained. "Nobody can tell us anything about it that we don't already know, and our frank opinion is that the complete abolition of strong drink would solve the problem of the world's happiness." With guilt-ridden conviction, Edwards wrote that "the *Eye Opener* has no defence to offer for the booze traffic. It is a bad business, none worse." Because of his support, and his tremendous influence, the Prohibition legislation was passed, and in 1916 Alberta became a dry province.

Humour and satire were Edwards's trademarks. The *Eye Opener* never pretended to cover legitimate news. It was a journal of social observation that increasingly became a platform for social commentary. It could, and did, make or break politicians. R.B. Bennett blamed his 1905 provincial defeat on Edwards. A Calgary mayor declined to run for re-election when Edwards opposed him. No public figure was immune from the *Eye Opener*'s attack. Inevitably, this sometimes led to legal action. When Edwards wrote that the "three biggest liars" in Alberta were "Robert Edwards, Gentleman, Hon. A. L. Sifton (premier) and Bob Edwards, editor of the *Eye Opener*," Premier Sifton promptly threatened libel. The suit was dropped when Edwards filed similar action on behalf of Robert Edwards, Gentleman, and Bob Edwards, Editor.

At one point, the Canadian Pacific Railway refused to let the *Eye Opener* be sold on its trains. Church ministers preached sermons of condemnation, but Edwards persisted. The only fight he could never win was against the bottle. "Every man has his favourite bird," he wrote. "Mine is the bat." When the *Eye Opener* failed to publish for several weeks, the whole town knew that Edwards was on the sauce. But his readers were always ready to forgive. "Had he lived longer, consumed less whisky, and possessed more ambition for personal advancement and fame, he might have shared immortal honours with the like of Mark Twain," wrote biographer MacEwan.

Lampooning politicians and social snobs was only one part of Edwards's attack on Canadian society. The "Robin Hood of the pen" was sympathetic to the plight of prostitutes, pushed for more relaxed divorce laws, spoke out against sweatshops, and fought the Sunday "blue" laws, which prohibited shops from opening on the Sabbath. He was far ahead of his time in matters of Senate reform, the environment, votes for women, hospitalization benefits, and old-age pensions. His columns were reprinted widely across Canada, in British and American newspapers, and in a book published by a Toronto firm under the title *Bob Edwards's Summer Annual.*

At age fifty-eight, Edwards married Kate Penman, a twenty-four-year-old Glasgow-born clerk who worked in R.B. Bennett's law office. Marriage was a struggle for the eccentric editor. It was not easy for him to accept meals at regular hours, and he would not or perhaps could not modify his drinking ways. But gradually he accepted his wedded status and liked it. "When a man is in love for the first time, he thinks he invented it," he said.

In 1921 Edwards set aside his traditional disdain for politicians to run as an independent in the provincial elections. He said it would give him a more effective pulpit for proclaiming his views on social reform. Edwards won a seat, but by the time he arrived in Edmonton, he was a sick man. He sat for only one session of the legislature and made only one speech, condemning the damning effects of the illegal liquor traffic and Prohibition, which he now opposed, having changed his opinion on the subject. It was a subject he knew well.

He died in November 1922 at age sixty-three, and the *Eye Opener* died with him. "One of the outstanding figures in freelance journalism in the Dominion of Canada," said the *Calgary Herald* obituary. As the editor of a journal with influence far beyond the boundaries of Calgary, Edwards had been the social conscience of his adopted country. He would have appreciated the irony of his dying only one year after becoming a politician. "Now I know what a statesman is," he had written. "He is a dead politician, and what this country needs is more of them."

The name of Bob Edwards lives on as the name of a fund-raising luncheon hosted by Calgary's Alberta Theatre Projects that has become the largest literary event in western Canada. Visiting speakers have included Margaret Atwood, Pierre Berton, and Mordecai Richler. The name of the *Eye Opener* lives on as the name of the local morning show heard on CBC Radio in Calgary. And the spirit of the *Eye Opener* lives on in the flimsy paper and cheap ink of *Frank*, a satirical Ottawa-based magazine that terrifies politicians, adulterers, and plagiarists from Halifax to Victoria. Edwards was a satirist who found much to lampoon. He would find a wealth of subjects today.

Henry Wise Wood
Farm leader
1860–1941

Henry Wise Wood was the first in a series of semi-mystical local visionaries—William Aberhart, Preston Manning, and Stockwell Day are some of the others—who have risen up when called upon to give voice to the concerns of western Canada. At a time when seventy percent of Albertans lived on the land, Wood was the most influential farm leader in this province. The premier's job was his for the asking when the United Farmers of Alberta swept to power in 1921, yet for reasons that remain unclear, Wood never sought political office. Instead, he expanded his role as farm leader and became a pivotal figure in the creation of wheat pools in Alberta.

Wood became an Albertan in 1905, the year Alberta became a province. Born in Missouri in 1860, just before the start of the American Civil War, he was the son of a prosperous farmer who owned properties in Missouri and Texas. As was customary in that place and time, his father was also a slave owner. Wood never saw this as being necessarily a bad thing. He said his father treated the slaves like family.

By the time he was a teenager, Wood was running his own cattle operation, and he became an early believer in agrarian reform. He supported the farm organizations that worked to protect the interests of the rural population, but he parted company with them when they entered politics.

He farmed until he was forty-five then, enticed by the opening of a new frontier, moved north to Alberta. In this new and undeveloped country, he hoped to find the democratic freedoms and economic security that farmers had started to lose in the United States during the depression of the 1890s. He bought a wheat farm near Carstairs and proclaimed his adopted home to be "the finest in the world."

When fellow farmers complained about having to accept what buyers chose to pay for their produce, Wood urged them to organize.

"You will never get anything in this world that you do not get for yourself," he said. He was active in the Society of Equity, an early farm organization that became part of the United Farmers of Alberta in 1909.

Wood became a Canadian citizen in 1911. "There is no use holding either a membership or citizenship unless one is going to use it," he said. Through his membership in the UFA, he pushed for the provincial government to organize the Alberta Co-operative Elevator Company, a farmer-owned grain elevator system designed to eliminate some of the commercial hazards of grain marketing.

Five years later Wood was elected president of the United Farmers of Alberta, and he became a dominant figure in the agricultural life of this province. He spent much of his time visiting UFA locals, preaching the need for a strong, broadly based union of farmers to deal with rural issues and counteract the growing power of bankers and industrialists. He did not believe that farmers should be directly involved in government. Instead, he thought they should develop a parallel organization to protect their interests.

By 1921, however, it had become clear to many farmers that having their own organization was not enough. Even though there were some thirty thousand farmers in the UFA, they did not have the collective power, it seemed, to make the government deal effectively with their economic and financial problems. So they formed themselves into a political party. Wood attempted to hold them back from this decision, but eventually he abandoned his opposition and choreographed the landslide that ended the Liberal regime and brought thirty-nine UFA candidates to the provincial legislature.

As UFA leader, Wood seemed the logical choice for premier when the farmers' party scored its political victory. But he turned down the keys to the premier's suite, and the job went instead to Herbert Greenfield, an English-born farmer from Westlock. Wood continued to play an active back-room role with the new political party while increasing his involvement in grain marketing issues.

The federal government had ended its control over grain marketing in 1920. Wood spearheaded the movement that established farmer-owned wheat pools throughout rural Alberta in 1923 and 1924 and later in Saskatchewan and Manitoba. "If the government will not provide a wheat board, the farmers can create their own," he said.

Between them, the three western pools eventually controlled the sales from 15 million acres of wheat and jointly represented the largest grower-controlled co-operative in the world. But co-operative buying and selling only went so far to protect farmers against economic hardship when the demand for wheat began to drop. Some said that the credit generated by their co-operative methods had to meet with a reciprocal monetary credit from the lending institutions before they could achieve economic stability. To this end, they began agitating for monetary reform.

Wood didn't think much of the monetary reformers, and he vented his feelings at one memorable UFA convention. Asked for his views on a resolution advocating an inquiry into the workings of Canada's money, he approached the chairman's table with clenched fist raised. "I know nothing about money, and I don't believe anyone else does," he shouted. "This question has been a hardy annual, and now it has become a noxious weed. My advice to you is to kill it." He then slammed his fist on the table. The motion was defeated, and all discussion of monetary reform was officially banned within the UFA. It was left to evangelist William Aberhart and his followers to promote the use of social credit as the means of rescuing the province and Canada from the drastic effects of the depression.

Wood served as president of the UFA until 1931 and as president of the Alberta Wheat Pool until 1937. By then he was seventy-seven and ready to retire to Carstairs. He died in 1941 at age eighty-one, leaving the farm to his three sons. Though born and raised an American, he had lived a typically Canadian life—he achieved great power and influence as a farm leader, yet turned down opportunities for greater glory and prestige, including a knighthood and the premiership of Alberta. When he died, his estate comprised little more than his farm property and a few hundred dollars.

In 1951 Wood became a member to the Alberta Hall of Fame, and his portrait was hung in the provincial legislature. A cairn honouring his memory was later installed in a Carstairs park, and in 1961 his name was given to the former Chinook High School in Calgary.

Chinook students were not impressed by the name change at

first. They complained that it would mean having to redesign their school crests and rewrite the school cheers. *Calgary Herald* columnist Andrew Snaddon commented that the name of Henry Wise Wood deserved to be known to all Albertans. "It is one the school can bear proudly, and one that future students could well live up to." In early 2000 some of those future students posted their resounding response to Snaddon's challenge on the school's Internet website: "We have!"

Victoria Calihoo

Buffalo hunter and folk historian

1861–1966

Victoria Calihoo was born at a time when buffalo still provided vital food and clothing for the people in her Métis community. She died the year before Canada celebrated its one hundredth birthday. Among her Cree-speaking people, stories were orally transmitted, rarely written down, and often lost to posterity. Fortunately, Victoria's stories have been collected and preserved in provincial archives. They offer a rare and fascinating insight into a way of life that had all but disappeared by the time she was in her early twenties.

Named after Queen Victoria and baptized by the Oblate missionary Father Albert Lacombe, Victoria grew up in Lac Ste. Anne, a Roman Catholic mission established by the Oblates northwest of Edmonton. She went on her first buffalo hunt when she was thirteen. Her Cree mother looked after the sick and injured on the hunt, and Victoria assisted her. Her mother was a medicine woman, skilled in the arts of setting broken bones and treating illnesses with medicinal herbs. The other women in the hunting party took care of skinning the buffalo carcasses, cleaning the hides, drying jerky, and feeding the hunters and children from the bountiful supply of fresh meat.

Hunters usually rode on horseback for two or three days before sighting the big herds. Women and children followed in tall-wheeled, ox-drawn carts known as Red River carts. The Métis travelled in large groups of one hundred or more because of the dangers of encountering hostile warriors along the way. "There were no police—no law," explained Victoria. They forded all rivers—including the formidable North Saskatchewan—pitched their tents on lands now occupied by the high-rise buildings of Edmonton, and rode home from the hunt happy and fulfilled, telling stories and singing songs.

The buffalo hunt was an important event in the life of the Métis of Alberta's northern communities because it provided them with the basic necessities. "It was a very useful animal," observed Victoria. "We ate the meat and we used its hide for robes, ropes, shelter for our wigwams, footwear, clothes, and bags." Dried buffalo dung substituted as an important source of fuel whenever firewood was in short supply. Only the bones, hoofs, and horns of the buffalo were discarded after a kill. Everything else found a practical use.

Victoria went on four buffalo hunts during her teens, and she recalled her sense of wonder at seeing her first herd. "It was just a dark, solid, moving mass," she said. "We, of those days, could never believe the buffalo would ever be killed off, for there were thousands and thousands." The spring hunt would occur after the Métis farmers had planted their vegetable gardens and sowed their fields, and the fall hunt took place after haying. It was considered the more important of the two. "We had to have enough dried meat and pemmican to last all winter." It was, she said, "the best and most nourishing food I ever had."

Buffalo meat, pemmican (cakes of powered dried meat bonded with melted fat), and fish were the staples of Victoria's childhood diet. She ate her meals on the floor because there were no chairs or tables in her house. She also slept on the floor because there were no beds. "Because we didn't have them, we didn't miss them." She never saw a candle or kerosene lamp until she was in her teens—flames from the fireplace provided her only light at night—and, in the absence of soap, washed herself with potash cleanser. "Perhaps it was rather hard for the delicate skin, but it was as good as any soap I have used."

Within thirty years, the buffalo were no more and the Red River cart became a symbol of a passing way of life. Victoria went on her last buffalo hunt around the time she was married, at age seventeen, to Louis Calihoo, a mixed-blood farmer with French, Cree, and Iroquois in his background. They raised twelve children, and Victoria contributed to the household income by working as a teamster with her husband. They drove freight for the Hudson's Bay Company between Fort Edmonton and Athabasca Landing. Louis later ran a sawmill and then a hotel at Lac Ste. Anne. He always kept the farm because Victoria said it was the best place to raise children.

Though Victoria had little formal education beyond the ability to read and write her own name, and her husband had no schooling at all, they saw education as the key to success for their children. They sent their six sons to a residential school southeast of Calgary and had their six daughters educated at a convent in St. Albert. Their grandchildren would hold university degrees and important public service jobs. The girl who went on buffalo hunts in her teens lived to see her descendants become professionals in the city.

Though lacking in education, Victoria was not without cultivated sensibilities. She owned one of the first player pianos in her part of the country. She was an early fan of music on the radio and renowned for the energy and skill she put into dancing the Red River Jig. In 1935, when she was seventy-four, she danced the jig at an Edmonton competition sponsored by the Northern Alberta Pioneers and Old Timers Association and walked away with the first prize of a tanned buffalo robe. On her one hundredth birthday, she astonished her family and friends by performing the jig "the way it should be done." She repeated the feat when she was 103.

Her husband died in 1926, when Victoria was sixty-five. She lived the rest of her life alone, never far from members of her expanding clan, which amounted to 241 descendants at the time of her death. She died in a seniors' home in St. Albert.

Victoria spoke mostly Cree until she was seventy-five, then worked on her English and started telling her stories for posterity. She saw two stories published in the *Alberta Historical Review*. One tells of her early life on the farm; the other recounts her vivid memories of the buffalo hunt.

She didn't have her first medical examination until she was ninety-nine. The doctor told her what she knew already—that she was in fine health. She attributed her long life to the fact that she never smoked or drank and never had to be treated by a physician. She used the medicines of nature, handed down to her by her mother.

"Behave yourself and work hard," she said. She lived past her 104th birthday, leaving behind a century of experiences, a century of memories. We can be grateful that she had them written down for future generations.

Henry Marshall Tory

University founder

1864–1947

The University of Alberta was founded in 1908 for the most pragmatic of reasons: to sell the young province to prospective settlers. The fact that many of the settlers might not actually use the new university mattered little to the provincial government of the time. The university would show the world just how far Alberta had come in the first three years of its existence.

The man the government chose to lead the university was cut from the same common-sense cloth as many of the settlers. Henry Marshall Tory was a down-to-earth man who thought an institution of higher learning should serve a practical purpose. He never envisaged building an ivory tower, an Oxford or Cambridge of the West. Tory, a Nova Scotia farmer's son, believed that an Alberta university should serve as a training centre for the sons and daughters of Alberta farmers who wanted to become lawyers or engineers or scientists.

His own training pointed him initially toward a career in religious education. Tory taught for a time at his local school in Guysborough, Nova Scotia, then trained for the Methodist ministry at McGill University. Hard-working and intelligent, he quickly obtained a faculty position at McGill. But his religious commitment wavered, and science and mathematics became his new academic specialties.

In 1905 Tory accepted the challenge to establish a McGill-affiliated college in Vancouver that eventually evolved into the University of British Columbia. Three years later he accepted an invitation from fellow McGill graduate Alexander Rutherford, the first premier of Alberta, to head the newly legislated provincial university in Edmonton.

The university's location was the subject of much controversy. Calgary, the larger of Alberta's two primary cities, had tried unsuccessfully to land the provincial university after Edmonton was chosen as the provincial capital in 1905. But Tory weathered the political storm and soon asserted the University of Alberta's control over the field of third-level education in the province.

The university opened for classes, in what is now Queen Alexandra School, with forty-five students and a faculty of five. Students could choose from classes in English, pure and applied mathematics, physics, literature, and modern languages. In his first convocation address, Tory said the university would play a practical role in the pioneer society "unhampered by fixed traditions" and "relating closely to the life of the people." The community it served would be the whole province, not just Edmonton.

From the beginning, Tory talked about "taking the university to the people" and he made community outreach one of his highest priorities. He logged thousands of miles visiting most of the towns and villages in the province. This was in the age before radio, and a visit from a "distinguished" professor ("they were all assumed to be distinguished," University of Alberta historian Doug Owram has cryptically noted) attracted much attention. The professor would give a lecture on history, literature, or physics, and this would be followed by a social event. A poster of the period describes a typical program: "Come and hear Dr. Broadus lecture on Shakespeare, and enjoy yourselves afterwards at a dance."

Within a few years, the university had its own campus in Edmonton's Strathcona area on the south bank of the North Saskatchewan River, near where coyotes howled at night. "Along with some four hundred students and two red brick buildings, we were the University of Alberta," wrote English professor R.K. Gordon. "And we felt sure that the future belonged to us, not to the coyotes."

Tory's personality dominated the new university. He disapproved of student organizations that were not open to all, and so did not permit fraternities and sororities. As a staunch Methodist, he was shocked when a new dance craze, the "one-step," hit the campus. A five-dollar fine was imposed on anyone caught performing it.

Tory's main reason for spending so much time on the road during the early years of the university was to ensure that the small province's limited resources for higher education would be committed only to the University of Alberta. He did not want to see a competing university established in Calgary. For that reason, he worked hard to convince the public that the University of Alberta could reach out to all the people of the province.

Tory took time away from the university in 1917 to establish the so-called "Khaki University" for Canadian soldiers stationed in England. He returned to Edmonton three years later and spent another eight years with the University of Alberta. During that time, the province grew steadily and so did the school.

In 1921 Tory created another institution for Alberta—Canada's first provincially funded science research council. He had been actively involved with a group of businessmen who expressed a need for such a facility and Tory, with his enthusiasm for building things, established what is now the Alberta Research Council. A few years later he took on the challenge of creating the National Research Council in Ottawa. When Tory was appointed president, the NRC had no funding, land, research staff, or laboratories. But that posed no problem for Tory. He had spent almost two decades turning paper institutions into practical facilities that politicians and the public wanted to support.

During his last years in Edmonton, Tory put the University of Alberta on a firmer footing, establishing a full-degree program in medicine and a bachelor of commerce program, and expanding the pharmacy program from a one-year diploma to a full degree. He also established a department of household economics, based on his belief that scientific techniques could make modern home life more comfortable. One of his final contributions to the university, in 1927, was a radio station, CKUA, which pioneered school broadcasts in the province before the schools even had radios. Local stores donated the receivers.

In 1928 Tory was ready to move on to his next building assignment, as full-time head of the National Research Council in Ottawa. He was then sixty-four, and the seven-year appointment put him well past retirement age. But the easy chair and the carpet slippers held no real appeal for Tory, especially when he felt that his work was not yet done. The depression had frustrated his attempts to make the NRC as strong an influence in Canada as the university had been in

Alberta, and Tory was quite bitter when the Conservative prime minister of the day, R.B. Bennett, chose not to renew his appointment.

His departure from the NRC forced him into retirement, but not for long. At age seventy-seven, he took on one final building challenge—he established Carleton College to meet the growing demand in Ottawa for adult education. At the time of his death, at age eighty-three, he was still active as unpaid president and lecturer. "Somehow it is hard to imagine Tory as an inactive pensioner," wrote historian Owram.

Little is known of Tory's personal life. His biographer, E.A. Corbett, relates that he did have a wife, the former Annie Frost, but says nothing more about his family life. Nor do we know what Tory did for hobbies or recreation.

The mystery deepens when one tries to determine why Tory abandoned his Methodist ministry at age forty to focus on science and university administration. After years of preaching in local churches, he announced that "I have never been able to find enough material on a religious theme to enable me to speak for more than fifteen minutes."

At the same time, as Owram has observed, there was perhaps as much missionary zeal in Tory's later work as there had been in his first calling: "In his commitment that education must be practical and serve the wider public, he was treating education the way he would treat religion. The greatest moral good it could serve was to reach the people. In this fashion, Henry Marshall Tory carried his sense of duty and his nineteenth-century Maritime upbringing to the twentieth century and to the development of Canadian education."

Richard Gavin Reid

Farmer and Alberta premier

1879–1980

History has consigned Richard Gavin Reid to political oblivion. His term as Alberta premier lasted just thirteen months—from July 1934 to August 1935—and ended with the annihilation of his United Farmers of Alberta government by William Aberhart's Social Credit juggernaut. Yet Reid's achievements in various UFA cabinet portfolios during the preceding thirteen years suggest that, had circumstances been different, he might have had more of an impact on the political scene. As it is, Reid is remembered only for two Guinness Book-style records: as the Alberta premier who served the shortest and lived the longest, 101 years.

Reid had the misfortune to be left with a crumbling and debt-ridden government in the midst of the depression. His predecessor, John Brownlee, had resigned amidst accusations of personal scandal orchestrated by his political opponents. Reid did not want to be premier, but he agreed to serve out the rest of Brownlee's term when the UFA's federal party president, Robert Gardiner, refused to leave his seat in the House of Commons and return to Alberta.

Reid accepted the premier's job with the acquiescence of a man born to serve. "My chief aim is to do my duty, wherever that may be," he said. "When duties are sent, powers are sent to enable their discharge."

Reid's first duty was sent in 1900, when he left his native Scotland at age twenty to fight in the Boer War as a member of the Royal Army Medical Corps. When he returned to Britain, he found the place much too stifling after the wide open spaces of South Africa. He decided to "strike out for a less crowded environment." With South Africa going through an unsettled period after the war, he chose western Canada "as the most desirable of the remaining locations available."

Reid landed in Manitoba in 1903 and worked as a farm labourer for fifteen dollars a month. A stint as a logger in Ontario followed and, when he tired of that, Reid headed toward Edmonton. For a down payment of $160, he took a homestead near the Scottish settlement of Scotstown, south of Mannville and east of the provincial capital. The 155-kilometre trip between his grain farm and Edmonton took fourteen days by horse-drawn wagon.

Because of his experience in the medical corps, Reid was called into service as the area's dentist. His wife, Marion, the farmer's daughter he married when he was forty and she was sixteen, recalled that some of his "patients" remained his best friends "so he couldn't have been too bad." But, she added, "I would never have let him pull a tooth of mine."

After serving as councillor and reeve at Buffalo Coulee, Reid became a local constituency president of the United Farmers of Alberta. When the farmers' lobby group became a political party and won the 1921 provincial election, Reid was elected MLA for Vermilion. He served as health minister in the cabinet of Herbert Greenfield and, when Brownlee replaced Greenfield, Reid became municipal affairs minister and then provincial treasurer. He also served as minister of lands and mines. When the federal government transferred ownership of resources to the provinces in 1930, he became Alberta's first minister of natural resources.

In July 1934 Brownlee resigned in the wake of a civil suit brought against him by a former government stenographer and her father. Reid's only comment on the so-called "Brownlee Affair" was that his boss had been framed, caught in a trap set by political opponents.

As premier, Reid presided over a single, turbulent legislative session. Drought- and depression-battered farmers needed economic assistance. Reid sought to find middle ground between the left-wingers in his party, who proposed joining the new Co-operative Commonwealth Federation, and the right wingers, who wanted to try the monetary reform theories being advanced by William Aberhart. Reid refused to support either option. He did not believe in socialism or in funny money theories. Two of his back-benchers registered their disappointment by crossing the floor to join the Liberals.

Although his UFA government brought in innovative debt adjustment legislation, Reid could not counteract the appeal of a radio evangelist who promised to throw the money changers out of the temple and pay a twenty-five-dollar monthly dividend to every citizen. Aberhart scored a stunning victory in the 1935 election. When the votes were counted, every member of the government, including Reid, had been drowned in the Social Credit deluge.

Reid left politics, worked briefly as a commission agent, then served on the federal government's mobilization board during the Second World War. In 1951, at age seventy, he embarked on a new career as librarian for Canadian Utilities in Edmonton. He worked a six-and-one-half-hour day "because I don't eat lunch." He had gained forty pounds after leaving farm work for politics, so he cut out lunch to stay in shape. Reid worked at Canadian Utilities until he was ninety-five and justified his long career by saying, "I had to have something to do and earn a living."

In January 1979, when he turned one hundred, Alberta's sixth premier received birthday greetings from Peter Lougheed, the province's tenth premier. What did he think of Lougheed? "Great vision, that broadening of Alberta's economic policy," replied Reid. "But he lets the Social Credit party and the NDP get away with too much." Reid said at the time that he owed his longevity to staying active. "Perhaps working until the age of ninety-five is part of the reason."

That was Reid's last public appearance. He died in October 1980, and Premier Lougheed was one of the people who paid their final respects at the brief cremation service.

J. Percy Page
Basketball coach and lieutenant governor

1887–1973

Commercial education teacher J. Percy Page had no particular interest in basketball when he reluctantly agreed in 1914 to coach the female students at Edmonton's McDougall Commercial High School. In fact, he only agreed to coach the McDougall girls when he lost a coin toss to the teacher who got the boys.

Page had played basketball without distinction while studying education at McGill and "I never took the game seriously," but he turned out to be a coach who could get results. He did so, in part, by being a stern disciplinarian. "Young ladies in my school do not slide down banisters," he told his charges. But his young ladies did shoot and pass. *00662-4166*

Page bought books about basketball techniques and devised a system of simple, well-executed shooting and passing plays. He entered his McDougall squad in a four-team school league and surprised everyone by winning the championship. "And we kept on winning," he said. "When our first class graduated, the girls asked me to keep a team going, and they became the Grads." The formal name of the team was the Commercial Graduates Basketball Club.

Page steered the Grads through 522 games over twenty-five years and saw them lose only twenty. In 1922 he brought them to Ontario to challenge the London Shamrocks for the Canadian title, which the Shamrocks had claimed without playing any teams from the West. The Edmonton women scored a one-sided victory and remained virtually undefeated at the national level until they disbanded in 1940.

The Grads' only national loss occurred in 1931, when the Canadian Amateur Basketball Association awarded the crown by default to the Toronto Lakesides. The Grads could not make the playoffs because they occurred outside the period that Page had booked off from his teaching job at McDougall. They did, however, challenge the Lakesides to play an exhibition series in Edmonton the

35

following year, and in the final game they trounced the Toronto team 120–20. "It was uncanny," said former Grads member Edith Sutton in a 1998 interview with an Ottawa newspaper. "Our fans so badly wanted to see Toronto humiliated."

Playing in an era in which most women's teams were engaged in six-a-side basketball—with three players from each team confined to half the court because it was believed that women did not have the muscle or the stamina to cover the full court—the Grads only played the modern five-person version of the game. Because of this, they were derided as "hoydens" (boisterous tomboys), a description that Sutton cheerfully accepted might have had some validity. "Some of them acted like that." But Page prohibited roughhousing. A stern disciplinarian, he demanded that "his girls" be ladies first, athletes second. Marriage brought an end to team membership. He also banned the girls from drinking, smoking, or "carrying on."

"He was desperate to keep us simon pure," said Sutton. "If you decided to show off, you got the 'look.' He never bawled us out."

In 1923 the Grads became champions at the international level, defeating a Cleveland team for the world basketball title. An Edmonton Chevrolet dealer was so happy that he presented coach Page with a new car. Page did not know how to drive but he quickly learned.

The Grads reigned as unofficial world champions for seventeen years. "The finest basketball team that ever stepped out on a floor," said James Naismith, the Canadian who invented the game. They also scored an unbeaten run of exhibition games at four summer Olympics although they had no corporate sponsorship for these appearances. Their efforts to have basketball sanctioned as an official women's medal sport were unsuccessful.

The Grads collected a total of 108 titles, from local to international levels, during their amazing twenty-five-year run. At the height of their fame, in 1930, they had packed an arena with 6,792 fans—a record for Canadian basketball. But fans gradually lost interest in a team that seemed virtually impossible to beat. At the end, their games drew barely a few hundred spectators.

The Grads played their last game just as Page's life was turning a new page. He retired from teaching bookkeeping, shorthand, and typing at McDougall and, at age fifty-three, he entered provincial politics as the independent member of the legislative assembly for Edmonton West. In 1952 he came back to win the riding for the Conservatives and served two terms as Tory house leader. He was defeated in the 1959 election and, later that year, became Alberta's eighth lieutenant governor.

Page remained in touch with the Grads long after their last game in 1940. He kept a list of the players and their current addresses in the top drawer of his desk in the lieutenant governor's office. He also kept all the many letters and cards they sent him. Every five years, Page and his wife Maude—who had served as the team's chaperone—organized a Grads reunion in Edmonton.

Page served as lieutenant governor until 1965. In his seventies, he was still as slim, ramrod straight, and dignified as he'd been in his coaching days. A friend described him as a man "standing on tiptoe, the better to discover what life is really all about." He died in March 1973 at age eighty-five. A month later, the Grads entered the Alberta Sports Hall of Fame. Three years after that, women's basketball became an official Olympic sport at the Summer Games in Montreal. In 1988 a National Film Board documentary called *Shooting Stars*, directed by the late Edmonton broadcaster Allan Stein, was released. The film won many awards and brought to the attention of a modern audience the achievements of one of the great sports teams in Canadian history and the reluctant coach who had put them on the world stage.

Chief Buffalo Child Long Lance

Celebrity fraud

1890–1932

The great appeal of the West for early settlers was that it gave them an opportunity for a fresh start. They could leave behind old baggage, try out new occupations, and try on new names. Whatever they had done before did not matter. The frontier looked to the future. Nobody dwelt on the past.

Usually it was sufficient for settlers just to forget. They could fashion a new identity without attaching a new biography to it. Only the most troubled of the newcomers saw a need to move beyond forgetting toward concocting a fictional past.

One such newcomer went by the name of Chief Buffalo Child Long Lance. Between the First and Second World Wars, he was the most famous Canadian Native after Grey Owl. Only trouble was, like the English-born Grey Owl, Long Lance was neither Canadian nor wholly Native. He moved to a new country and transformed his identity.

Long Lance's real name was Sylvester Long. He was the son of mixed-blood parents who lived in the black section of Winston-Salem, North Carolina. He was part white and part Cherokee, and could well have been part black as well. The apartheid of the time and place branded him as "coloured," and his prospects were not good. At the age of twelve he ran away from home, joined a Wild West show, and began his masquerade as a Cherokee.

Through chutzpah and deceit, he entered a Pennsylvania residential school for Natives and then a small military college in upstate New York. Then he took the train to Montreal and, using the name Sylvester Long Lance, embarked for Europe as a member of the Princess Patricia's Canadian Light Infantry serving with the Canadian Expeditionary Force. He fought at Vimy Ridge, suffered injuries in battle, and worked in army intelligence as a sergeant. He later claimed the rank of lieutenant and the award of a *Croix de Guerre* for bravery—both false.

After his discharge in 1919, Long Lance moved to Calgary, where his lies would not catch up with him right away. He joined the *Calgary Herald* as a reporter, pretending to be both a Blackfoot chief from Oklahoma as well as a West Point-trained war hero.

Notwithstanding the fact that he was living a lie, Long Lance proved to be a reliable and generally credible reporter. He covered all the news of the day, from police to sports to city hall, and did some fine work covering Native life on the reserves around Calgary. One of his most striking efforts was an account of the devastating impact of tuberculosis on the Sarcee reserve during the early 1920s. The Bloods, part of the Blackfoot confederacy, adopted him as an honorary chief and gave him the name Buffalo Child.

Long Lance lived and worked in Calgary for just three years, until he became bored with newspaper work. The city hall beat gave him little to cheer about, with its stories about poverty relief agencies, property taxes, and sewer line extensions.

To liven things up, Long Lance concocted a prank that would cost him his job and guarantee his place in *Herald* newsroom lore. Posing as a gas inspector, he put on a gas mask, rolled a fuse-lit "bomb" into council chambers, and wrote a story so rich in insider detail that he was quickly fingered as the culprit. The mayor tried to intercede on his behalf, but *Herald* management refused to listen. Long Lance became the first and only reporter in *Herald* history to have his firing recorded on the newspaper's front page.

Long Lance then headed for Vancouver, where he persuaded the *Sun* to let him write an article about the coastal Natives of British Columbia. After that, he moved to Regina, and wrote about the Saskatchewan Natives, followed by a move to Winnipeg, where he wrote about the Manitoba Natives. By then, he had given himself a new ethnic background and was presenting himself as a Canadian Blood Native to "give my writings an additional touch of interest."

Long Lance returned to Calgary in 1923, staged a mock kidnapping of the mayor as a publicity stunt, and so impressed the people running the Calgary Exhibition and Stampede that they offered him a public relations job. The following summer found him in Banff doing publicity for the CPR resort hotels. Then it was on to the bright lights of New York and Los Angeles, where, trading on his Blackfoot name, he carved out a lucrative career as a celebrity Native—a full-time noble savage. Dressed in the regalia of a Blackfoot chief, he lectured widely, attended the best parties, and rubbed shoulders with Hollywood royalty. His dark hair, sallow skin, and prominent cheekbones made the deception possible. Like Grey Owl, he looked the part.

By 1926 American newspapers were referring to "Chief Buffalo Child Long Lance" as the "big boss" of all the Indian tribes on the great Canadian plains. Long Lance had left Alberta behind, though he did return to "research" his "autobiography."

His fictional life story, published in 1928, became a best seller. Long Lance followed it by starring in a feature film, *The Silent Enemy*, about Ojibwa life in the forests of northern Canada.

But his past and his lies were starting to catch up with him— unlike Grey Owl, he had left too many loose ends. The U.S. Indian Affairs Bureau, acting on a tip, looked into his background, suspecting fraud. An anthropologist denounced his "autobiography" as a fake. The movie lawyers accused him of being an impostor and threatened to sue, only withdrawing their objections when Long Lance convinced them he was at least part Native.

By 1932 Long Lance could no longer keep living a lie. His life had become a kind of art with himself as the final text. Canada had allowed him to wear new clothes, but now people could see through them to the fraud underneath. He had spent more than half his life lying, covering up his tracks, then lying some more to cover up the previous lies. The strain became too much for someone who had never truly lived by the identity he wore. Long Lance started drinking, became reclusive, then shot himself in the head.

He was forty when he killed himself at a posh Hollywood ranch owned by a patron of Native culture and was buried at a war veterans' cemetery in Los Angeles. People say his ghost still haunts the place where he died. The mansion was later featured in the *Fantasy Island* television series. Could the producers have known about its long-ago connection to a professional Native who had lived his life as a fantasy?

Although he enters the history books as a fraud—"the glorious impostor," as his Calgary biographer, Donald B. Smith, calls him— Long Lance should also be remembered for making some positive contributions. At a time when Canadian Natives suffered even worse discrimination than blacks in the American South, Long Lance stepped forward to make them feel good about their ethnic heritage. Because of him, people began to treat with respect the Bloods, the Blackfoot, and the Cree. In Alberta this troubled fugitive from the truth found a place where, for the first time in his life, he could truly feel at home.

Kathleen Parlow

Violin virtuoso

1890–1963

In 1963 the concertmaster of the Calgary Philharmonic—a woman named Mary Williams—said in a newspaper interview that she considered herself a rarity in Canada. She did not know of any other female orchestra leaders, nor could she recall there ever having been any. "They only use women when they can't get men," she said.

Williams must have forgotten that the leader of Calgary's very first orchestra was a woman named Kathleen Parlow. Williams had even performed with Parlow. They had played in concerts together in Toronto during the 1940s, after Williams had graduated from the University of Alberta and started to make her way in the music world.

Parlow was a brilliant musician. Born in 1890 in Calgary, where her father worked for the Hudson's Bay Company, she started playing the violin at age four, and right from the start was destined to make her name internationally. She trained in San Francisco and Leningrad, gave her first recital at age six, and by age fifteen was performing for the British Royal family. She made her professional debut in Berlin in 1907, then toured the world as a concert soloist.

Parlow left her biggest mark in Toronto, where she was a frequent soloist with the Toronto Symphony. She performed with some of the most prominent Canadian artists of the period, including a young pianist named Mario Bernardi, who later achieved renown as the conductor of the National Arts Centre orchestra and of the Calgary Philharmonic. Parlow was also well known as the founder of the acclaimed Parlow String Quartet, which achieved an international reputation during its run from 1943 to 1958.

While Toronto gave her the outlet she needed for her great talent, Parlow always thought of Calgary as home. The only reason she never came back to Calgary to live was that the city held too many bitter memories for her mother. Her father had died of tuberculosis contracted from a Native woman, and her mother had vowed that she would never allow her daughter to be tainted by the scandal.

Calgary, nevertheless, was always happy to welcome Parlow back for short visits. When her first North American concert tour brought her to the city in 1910, she received the kind of welcome reserved for visiting royalty. The morning *Albertan* reported that, around the world, the twenty-year-old violin virtuoso was judged "not as a woman but as an artist." The men in her profession, said the *Albertan,* "have declared that she is today one of the phenomena of the musical world." She played the Shriners' Hall to an enraptured crowd of 638 who called for three encores and showered her with floral bouquets. "Time after time, Miss Parlow had to bow her acknowledgments with infinite sweetness," reported the *Albertan.* An admirer said she could sustain the notes beautifully, "as if she were playing with a nine-foot bow."

Parlow returned to Calgary the following year ("the concert went very well with almost too much applause," said Parlow's biographer, Maida Parlow French) and helped launch the city's first symphony orchestra, a seventeen-piece string ensemble. She had her photograph taken with the orchestra, then led members through their first performances before resuming her concert career. During this time she also encouraged participation in the Calgary Women's Musical Club, a concert organization founded in 1904 by singer Jeanette Sharples to bring "the warmth of music to an ever-growing population at a time when entertainment is lacking in this city." The Women's Musical Club brought classical music to such venues as the Palliser Hotel ballroom and the Victoria Pavilion.

Parlow returned to Calgary many times during her international concert career, which ended with a nervous collapse in 1927. Later visits included a trip in 1956 to receive the University of Alberta's prestigious National Award in Music at the Banff School of Fine Arts and what turned out to be her last visit in 1960, to adjudicate at a music festival.

That final visit was a most unhappy experience for the distinguished Canadian musician, then seventy years old. She tripped over a lamp cord in her room at the Palliser Hotel, fell heavily, and broke her left arm from shoulder to elbow. She did recover sufficiently—

after surgery in Toronto—to resume playing and lecturing, but her travelling days were over. She gave her final recital at age seventy-one and died of a heart attack two years later, in August 1963.

Thanks to her recordings, scholarships, and two generations of students, Parlow's influence continues to be felt throughout Canada and the world. And while her links with Alberta's musical history may have been sporadic and short-lived, she still deserves at least a footnote in the program.

As for Parlow's former playing partner Mary Williams, she served as concertmaster of the Calgary Philharmonic for fourteen years. When English conductor Maurice Handford took over the orchestra in 1970, she moved one chair to the left to become associate concertmaster.

Williams and several other musicians left the orchestra one year later amid newspaper reports of a "musicians' revolt" against Handford's dictatorial leadership. Williams said she just needed time off to recharge her batteries and added that she looked forward to the change of being in the audience during the following concert season. She soon faded quietly into the background of Calgary's music life. Williams died in June 1995.

Morris Shumiatcher
Cowboy hat manufacturer
1892–1958

The story of Morris Shumiatcher is the tale of every immigrant who ever came to Alberta, stayed, and prospered. Immigrants built our province. They chose Alberta as their home and set the foundations for their children and grandchildren to build upon. They lived in exile, and they fed on dreams of hope.

Morris was one of a large family of dispossessed Russian Jews who came here during the first part of the 1900s to escape persecution. They were part of a mass migration that lasted from the 1880s to the beginning of the Second World War.

Morris was the second of eleven children, born on a rental farm in the Gomel region of what would later become the Soviet republic of Byelorussia. Liberal land laws introduced by Czar Alexander II had made it possible for Russian Jews to rent farms and timber rights and to contemplate lives of freedom and prosperity. However, when the czar was assassinated in 1881, false rumours of Jewish involvement incited Russian mobs to attack Jews and destroy their property.

The Shumiatchers were driven from their farm by anti-Semitic thugs with clubs and torches. The father, Judah Shumiatcher, became a tradesman in the lumbering town of Gomel but could not find the means to support his wife and children.

Alberta beckoned as the family's salvation. A friend named Solomon Malkin had already moved to Calgary, where he earned a modest living selling groceries and fruit. He sent word back to the Shumiatchers that Alberta was "a land flowing with milk and honey."

Morris urged his father to move the family to Alberta. He had seen posters in the Gomel post office advertising farmland that could be bought cheaply, through the help of Jewish philanthropic organizations, at Jewish-run agricultural colonies in western Canada. The area north and east of Calgary was said to be particularly rich in grain-growing land.

Judah was hesitant. What if the advertisements turned out to be misleading? The Shumiatchers could not have known it at the time, but a Canadian Pacific Railway promotional brochure then circulating in the United States declared, "The country is one of pleasant temperatures, with very little snowfall. Sleighs are seldom, if ever, used in southern Alberta."

Judah struck a deal with his second son—he would give Alberta a try for one year. If things worked out, he would bring over the rest of the family. If not, he would return to Gomel. Eldest son Abraham would remain behind to help his mother look after the other nine children while Judah and Morris tried their luck in Canada.

Morris, then seventeen, agreed to the one-year deal, and father and son left Gomel in 1909. When they arrived in Canada, they registered for two sections of land near what is now the town of Rumsey, northwest of Drumheller.

The language barrier proved to be a problem when Judah and Morris tried to communicate with the government official who took down their particulars. "How about something simpler, beginning with 'S,'" suggested the officer as he struggled with the name Shumiatcher. "How about Smith?" Judah and Morris agreed, and so they began their new life in Canada with a name that gave no hint of their Jewish history or culture.

The name change, at that point, was no problem for Morris. "He thought it was a good idea," his son Judah recalled later, "that to come over was a good start, a new land, and what's wrong with a new name?"

Judah and Morris spent their first Canadian winter in a sod hut on their new property. During the one year of their Alberta farming experiment, they produced a good crop of grains and made some money, but the remoteness of the area was a problem. On their Gomel farm, the Shumiatchers had lived close to a metropolitan centre with synagogues, schools, and business opportunities. They needed to be closer to the city.

Father and son did not return to Gomel, though, as they had initially agreed. Instead, they decided to try their luck in Calgary. In 1910 they became part of the city's small community of Jewish immigrants, which then numbered six hundred. The rest of the

Shumiatcher family arrived in Canada the following year. Judah became Calgary's first Hebrew teacher, instructing classes in a room at Central School on Fifth Avenue East. Morris worked in a sawmill but harboured dreams of becoming an actor in the emerging California movie industry.

Morris hitchhiked to Hollywood to pursue his dream. Although he found work as a silent film extra, the fast-paced movie lifestyle did not suit him, and the money he made was little more than he could earn in a Canadian sawmill. After one year in the movie business, he returned to Calgary and enlisted in the Canadian army. He spent the First World War years stationed in Alberta.

After the war Morris decided his wandering days were over. He would stay in Canada and contribute to his adopted country as a producer of something, though he didn't yet know what. A growing country needed producers, he said. He visited Calgary's new public library, which an Ontario transplant named Alexander Calhoun had opened before the war, and looked through the picture books in search of inspiration. After seeing photographs of hats and then reading up on hat manufacturing, he decided what he would produce.

A cleaning and blocking plant named Calgary Hat Works provided Morris with his opportunity. With a down payment of $300, he could acquire the plant and convert it into a hat manufacturing and retailing operation. Because he had no collateral, the bank refused to lend him the money and suggested he ask his younger brother Harry—who owned a successful magazine and newspaper retail business called Harry's News and Tobacco Shop—to back him. Morris was indignant. If his signature wasn't good enough, then forget it. "But the next day he was back," recalled his son. "He had reconsidered and, of course, Harry did sign for him, and he had the $300. Within a year, he was making hats." Morris named his company Smithbilt Hats.

When the company was established, Morris met Ette Shector, an immigrant from Romania who had come to Calgary with her mother and four siblings during the 1920s. Morris had found a job for her at the request of his older brother, Abraham, a multilingual lawyer who helped newly-arrived immigrants in Calgary. The connection eventually blossomed into love and marriage.

For the first twenty-five years of its existence, Smithbilt Hats made and sold fedoras for men. Morris ran the factory, and its associated retail stores in Alberta, Saskatchewan, and British Columbia, from the tough times of the depression through the Second World War. After the war, the demand for fedoras declined, and Morris switched to producing cowboy hats.

Though he retained the name Smith for business purposes, Morris decided to revert privately to Shumiatcher. His friends told him he was crazy. "It's the wrong thing to do," they said. "Everyone knows you as Morris Smith. Besides, you have Smithbilt Hats."

Morris eventually relented and changed his name back to Smith, but only for a few years. By 1946 he was calling himself Morris Shumiatcher again.

His children went through a form of identity crisis with every name change. His daughter Clara said she had a different last name in every grade—Shumiatcher in Grade three, Smith in Grade four. "It's a wonder I never got a complex."

In the summer of 1946, Morris made a business decision that would guarantee him a lasting place in the Canadian history books. Hats in light pastel colours were all the rage at the time because they had been unavailable during the war. With the Calgary Stampede coming up, Morris ordered enough white felt to make eighteen cowboy hats. "This is a first," he noted. "Even the good guys in the movies don't wear pure white hats—just pastels." A Calgary rancher and oilman named Bill Herron Jr. bought four of the white hats for him and his family to wear in the Stampede parade. The rest sold out that same afternoon.

The following year, Smithbilt made 240 hats for the Stampede trade. They sold as fast as the original eighteen. "It was strictly on a hunch," said Judah Jr. "The population just grabbed them. And so it was established, in 1947, that the white hat was a winner."

In 1948 the white Smithbilt hat went national when a rowdy crowd of three hundred Calgarians wore the hats to the Grey Cup game in Toronto. Don Mackay, a Calgary broadcaster turned alderman, was the civic booster who had suggested wearing the white hats to the Grey Cup. When he became mayor in 1949, he donned his white Smithbilt hat and red tie and, in the words of a friend, "set out to convert the whole world to Calgarianism." He began offering the white hats as gifts to visiting celebrities, starting a tradition that continues to this day.

By the time Mackay left office ten years later, the hat that Smith built had become an internationally recognized symbol of western hospitality. Thanks to the business acumen of Morris Shumiatcher Smith, Calgary had become perhaps the only city on the planet to adopt a hat as its civic symbol.

Morris kept the Smithbilt name synonymous with the best in quality western hats until he died—a proud Shumiatcher—in 1958.

His legacy endures in the labour-intensive Smithbilt operation, which has changed little in more than sixty years. There are no assembly lines or computerized machines at the plant. Each hat is steamed, stretched, and shaped by hand, one at a time. "There's no substitute for hand labour," said manager Isaac Apt.

Smithbilt is the official supplier for the Professional Rodeo Association, the Calgary Stampede, and the Calgary Convention and Visitors Bureau, which—continuing the practice started by Mayor Mackay—gives away between eight thousand and ten thousand hats every year. The hats have adorned the heads of such people as Jean Chretien, Mikhail Gorbachev, Wayne Gretzky, and a host of Hollywood stars. When the Duke of Edinburgh received his third white hat, he feigned dismay and remarked, "Oh, not another one!"

Had he lived to see it, Morris Shumiatcher would likely have been embarrassed by the fuss surrounding the presentation in April 1999 of a ceremonial white Smithbilt hat to Zhu Rongji, the Chinese premier. More than one hundred pro-Tibetan protesters—some wearing black cowboy hats—shouted anti-Zhu slogans and said he didn't deserve a hat.

But Morris's heart would have swelled with pride to see the Canadian athletes marching onto the snow-covered field at McMahon Stadium, waving their white Smithbilt hats, during the opening ceremonies of the 1988 Calgary Winter Olympics.

"I'll never forget the look of the Canadian team walking into the stadium with their white hats on," said Judah Jr. "They looked so handsome. And they were. They created a tremendous impact all over the world."

Eric Harvie
Philanthropist
1892–1975

Eric Harvie was one of the most generous donors of cultural objects this country has ever seen. In 1966 he gave his entire collection of artworks and artifacts—more than two hundred thousand objects in all—to the people of Alberta. The collection, together with a $5-million endowment from Harvie, was used to start what is now the Glenbow Museum, a cultural institution with an international reputation for exhibitions, programs, and publications. The gift was the first of many offerings that the magpie millionaire gave to his community. He was, as *Time* magazine said, a "rich man who gave everything back and then some."

Harvie collected everything that appealed to him, which was just about anything imaginable. "It seemed every time he went on vacation, he'd rape an island," said his one-time law partner George Crawford. From his various trips abroad, Harvie shipped back to Calgary such garage sale exotica as the last Model T ever built, a set of Queen Victoria's royal bloomers, and the drum that sounded at Sitting Bull's command before the Battle of the Little Bighorn. When Harvie took a trip to Egypt, an assistant quipped, "I wonder where we'll put the pyramids." Although the pyramids never left the Middle East, enough other Harvie acquisitions did to fill several warehouses in Calgary.

He started collecting things after making his fortune in oil. A dentist's son from Orillia, Ontario, Harvie was working as a corporate lawyer in Calgary during the 1940s when a cash-strapped rancher client offered him the mineral rights to vast tracts of north-central Alberta land as payment for a $30,000 billing.

When the big Leduc oil strike occurred in 1947, Harvie held the rights to 486,000 acres of adjacent property. That, combined with the leases he held in the Vermilion and Redwater fields, made him rich.

By the early 1950s, he was worth an estimated $100 million, a figure quoted in newspapers at the time. When Harvie complained to Alberta Mines Minister Allen Patrick about the press speculating on the value of his holdings, the minister asked him if the news stories were inaccurate. "You know," replied Harvie, "I've never really thought about that." Harvie spent just eight years making money in the oilpatch. After that, he dedicated himself entirely to collecting and charitable giving.

Author Peter C. Newman says Harvie was perhaps "the only rich Canadian who leaves behind a popular legacy. His instinct for collecting anything and everything he happened to see endowed his foundations with the finest collection of western artifacts and general trivia anywhere."

The Glenbow—named after Harvie's ranch—was formed by an act of the provincial legislature to accommodate and keep tabs on the returns from the millionaire's various trips to estate sales and auctions around the world. Harvie hired archaeologist Dick Forbis, an expert on the Natives of the northern plains, to sort out the artifacts relating to Native culture before white settlers arrived in the Americas. Art expert Moncrieff Williamson indexed and graded the paintings, drawings, sculptures, and photographs Harvie acquired, while librarian Pat McCloy catalogued and shelved boxes of rare books, posters, pamphlets, and programs.

As well as sorting the materials, staff were also under orders to increase the collections. As historian Hugh Dempsey said, "We were told to go out and collect like a bunch of drunken sailors." But unlike Harvie, who indiscriminately picked up artifacts from anywhere he wanted, employees were limited to acquiring pieces related primarily to western Canadian history.

Because of his public generosity, a wealth of Canada's natural history and archaeology has been preserved. "To neglect history is one of the shortcomings of civilization," said Harvie. To compensate for this neglect in Alberta, he gave the province millions of dollars to support art and historical collections, preserve Canadiana, and finance parks, gardens, and scientific research.

Money from his foundation has gone to the Banff Centre, the Confederation Centre in Charlottetown, the Calgary Zoo, Canada

Olympic Park, the riverbank pathways in Calgary, and dozens of other projects. Harvie was the unnamed benefactor responsible for both the bronze equestrian statue of Robert the Bruce outside Calgary's Jubilee Auditorium and the statue of General Wolfe outside the Centennial Planetarium. He also gave money to many Alberta towns to spruce up their main streets.

"Mr. Harvie is one of those men who has been endowed with a sense of history, and he has the energy and ability to do something about it," said the citation that came with his 1957 honorary doctorate from the University of Alberta.

Harvie chose to keep his good deeds quiet. Very few of his gifts have his name attached to them, although one notable exception is the Eric Harvie Theatre at the Banff Centre. Today the Devonian Group of Charitable Foundations continues to give bequests from his estate. About $30 million of the $75 million total has been given to Calgary, with the rest going to park and river pathways in other western Canadian cities. "They have done wonders for western Canada," said a parks official in Calgary. "Everywhere you look, there are big chunks of Harvie family money planted."

In contrast to his public generosity, Harvie's personal spending habits were those of a frugal middle-class businessman. He always lived in the same modest bungalow in Elbow Park that he had bought when he was a young lawyer, and he rejected the Cadillac— the traditional status symbol of the oilpatch—in favour of a battered old Studebaker.

Harvie died in January 1975 at age eighty-two. Like the older breed of Canadian millionaires, and like many who have lived in Calgary, he had never sought publicity during his life. Because he had done much of his charitable work semi-anonymously, his name soon faded into obscurity.

Harvie rarely granted media interviews, but shortly before his death he did agree to lift the veil slightly and talk to author Peter C. Newman about aspects of his career. "Out of the fullness of his life," said Newman, "he was willing to impart only one sage bit of advice: 'Never throw away old socks, old underwear, or old cars.'"

Jock Palmer

Radio and aviation pioneer

1895–1964

The call letters for the radio station are CJOC. Lethbridge old-timers pronounce it "C-Jock," remembering Jock Palmer, the man who founded the station in 1926.

Palmer is remembered both as a Lethbridge radio pioneer and as an aviation pioneer. Born in Cambridge, England, he moved to Lethbridge with his parents in 1905 when he was nine. At age nineteen, he enlisted for wartime army service. He received the distinguished conduct medal for action in France with the Second Brigade, Machine Gun Company, and was promoted from corporal to lieutenant. He then joined the Royal Flying Corps, earned his wings, and spent the rest of the war flying reconnaissance missions over the trenches of France.

An amateur radio enthusiast since before the First World War, Palmer is credited with helping design and test an air-to-ground wireless communication system for the Royal Flying Corps. He remained with the air force for two years after the war, flying British aircraft from the war zone back to England. He was forced to ditch two of the planes in the English Channel. On the first occasion, he swam to shore. On the second, he bailed out and was rescued.

Discharged from the services with the rank of captain, Palmer returned to Lethbridge, went into partnership with fellow air force veteran Harry Fitzsimmons, formed the Lethbridge Aircraft Company, and bought a two-seater, single-engine Curtiss Jenny biplane for barnstorming.

No one hears much about barnstorming nowadays, but during the 1920s and 1930s, it was a popular entertainment attraction throughout North America. Pilots presented stunt-flying demonstrations at county fairs and exhibitions and paid for their fuel by taking customers on short five-dollar rides. Barnstorming never offered much of a living, but it helped pilots build up hours and experience.

For the next two years, Palmer and Fitzsimmons thrilled Lethbridge residents with their aerobatics and wing-walking displays over the city. In June 1922 they made international headlines when they attempted North America's first government-sanctioned air mail flight, from Lethbridge to Ottawa, with nine planned service stops in Canada and the United States along the way. The trip was abandoned after three days. Palmer wrecked the plane while attempting a landing in Minot, North Dakota. He swerved to avoid a car driven by a student using the landing field for driving practice, ran the plane's undercarriage into the ground, and sheared off both wings. The mail went on to Ottawa by train. Palmer and Fitzsimmons shipped back the remains of their damaged aircraft by truck and travelled home by train.

When they arrived in Lethbridge, they discovered they had become celebrities. The *New York Herald* had written a long story commending the Lethbridge fliers for attempting the continent's first airmail flight authorized by the Postmasters General in both Canada and the United States. The letters carried by Palmer and Fitzsimmons became collectors' items. Sold for one dollar apiece and bearing a three-cent postage stamp, the envelopes contained the message: "Greetings via the First Canadian Air Mail Plane from Lethbridge, Alberta: The Little City with the Big Future."

Palmer and Fitzsimmons were unable to repair their plane, and the Lethbridge Aircraft Company went out of business. Two years later, in 1924, they decided to give commercial aviation another try. They formed Southern Alberta Air Lines, and offered round-trip passenger service between Lethbridge and Waterton Lakes for thirty-five dollars. "Millions now walking will sometime fly" was their slogan.

Their second aviation venture ended after just three months. Palmer ran the plane into a badger hole while attempting a takeoff in Pincher Creek. The plane was damaged further in the attempt to remove it from the accident scene. Fitzsimmons quit the aviation business for good, and Palmer turned his attention to broadcasting.

After a few unsanctioned radio transmission experiments, Palmer applied for Lethbridge's first broadcast licence. In partnership with Harold Carson, a Lethbridge car dealer, and W. W. Grant, a Calgary engineer, he started CJOC with one announcer and a fifty-watt transmitter. The station went on the air in 1926, broadcasting for one to two hours daily.

CJOC quickly expanded. In 1928 it moved to the penthouse of Lethbridge's Marquis Hotel and doubled its power to one hundred watts. Programming increased to four and one-half hours daily. Carson bought out his partners, and Palmer returned to aviation as a pilot for Lethbridge Commercial Airways, taking passengers on short sightseeing trips at $7.50 per ride.

After one flying season, Palmer left Lethbridge Commercial Airways and moved to Calgary, where he flew a plane for the Lethbridge Brewing Company, advertising the brewery's Purple Label beer. Over the next dozen years, he worked for a succession of flying services operating out of Calgary, ran a flying school in Windermere Valley, and flew forestry patrols in the mountains of British Columbia.

With the outbreak of the Second World War, Palmer re-enlisted in the armed services as a flight instructor and helped spearhead southern Alberta's involvement in the British Commonwealth Air Training Plan. He instructed at the RCAF's No. Five Elementary Flying Training School, initially based at Kenyon Field in Lethbridge. Then he moved with the school to High River. "The high winds in Lethbridge kept the planes more on the ground than in the air," explained Palmer's fellow instructor Bill Smith. In 1944 Palmer received the Air Force Medal, the RCAF's top training award, for "valuable service rendered as a flying instructor."

After the war Palmer remained in High River, where he ran an electrical business and continued to add to his flying hours log as a member of the High River Flying Club.

In June 1962, on the fortieth anniversary of his pioneering air-mail flight, Palmer was honoured at a banquet sponsored by the High River Rotary Club. He recalled some of the mechanical troubles he had encountered with his planes during his early years in aviation and commented, "I'd go home if they asked me to take one of those things up today."

Palmer died in November 1964 at age sixty-eight. "He was a man of vision and determination whose work brought comfort, security, and belief to both those fields—radio and aviation—which he pioneered and loved," said the presiding minister at his funeral.

Palmer was inducted into Canada's Aviation Hall of Fame in 1988. "His pioneering work in the use of air to ground wireless, his piloting the first international air mail run, and his continued dedication to instructing others to fly have been of outstanding benefit to Canadian aviation," said the accompanying citation.

The radio station that the old-timers call "C-Jock" continues to serve the listeners of Lethbridge and area, offering "good times and great country favourites." Among aviation enthusiasts, Palmer is remembered as someone who believed there was a future for a machine that could fly through miles of empty air. Among radio enthusiasts, he is remembered as someone who believed there was a future for a type of entertainment that could transmit through miles of empty air. Palmer Park in Lethbridge and Palmer Road in Calgary are named in his memory.

Betty Mitchell
Community theatre pioneer
1896–1976

For most Albertans, prior to the 1930s, theatre was something that came from someplace else. If you wanted to see a play, you had to wait for the Chautauqua or one of the other travelling shows that brought European and American culture to this part of the world.

Only in Edmonton, where the Edmonton Little Theatre was formed in 1929, did community theatre have any kind of foothold. Elsewhere in the province, locally produced theatre did not emerge as a recognized feature of community life until the arrival of Betty Mitchell. She was an Ohio-born high school teacher with a passion for the stage who showed Canadians they could do their own theatre and do it well. While associated primarily with Calgary, she left an impact on community theatre throughout southern Alberta.

At the University of Alberta, where she studied science in the 1920s, Mitchell worked with the dramatic society and recalled that English professors, "drunk on words," ran it as a kind of elocution program. Their stage productions had more to do with the cult of the voice beautiful and the felicities of poetic language than with power of dramatic presentation.

Mitchell had not seen much theatre before attending university. The daughter of an alcoholic newspaperman who abandoned the family when she was fourteen, she moved to Canada with her mother, sister, and brother at age sixteen. Mitchell suffered from a bad cough, and doctors advised her mother they should move to a drier climate for the sake of the child's health. The family lived for seven years on a small farm near Oyen. After she finished high school, which she took by correspondence, Mitchell moved to Calgary to train as a teacher at normal school, then to Edmonton for university.

Mitchell directed a few productions for the University of Alberta Dramatic Society and learned much from the experience. She discovered that while her acting talent was limited and she knew virtually nothing about theatrical techniques, she did have a gift for inspiring other actors to shine. "Place yourselves in my hands," she said, and the actors responded accordingly.

When she returned to Calgary, Mitchell helped establish a group known as the Green Room Club, which had the rather lofty aim of promoting theatre throughout the province. She spent her days teaching English and algebra and her evenings reading and discussing plays with fellow drama enthusiasts.

At the Side Door Playhouse, the Green Room Club staged plays in which Mitchell participated both as actor and director. Despite her protests that she was a terrible actress, she earned good reviews.

The Green Room Club organized the first Alberta Drama Festival in 1930, and four community theatre groups—one each from Calgary, Edmonton, Lethbridge, and Medicine Hat—took part. Two years later, Calgary sent three troupes to the festival. Mitchell's influence had led to an explosion of amateur theatre in the city. Calgary, in fact, had more active theatre groups than the city could practically support.

In 1932 the various theatre groups joined forces under an umbrella group, the Calgary Theatre Guild, which coordinated the actors and backstage crews and worked to ensure there would be audiences for the plays. Mitchell staged several plays for the Guild, consolidating her reputation as a director.

When the Alberta high school curriculum was revamped to include drama in 1935, Mitchell, who was teaching algebra at Western Canada High, was named head of the new department. "Drama was such a fascinating subject," she said. "I often worked eighteen hours a day." She had no academic training for the task, having studied English, mathematics, botany, and agriculture at university. But she had the books and the desire.

One of her students from that period recalled that Mitchell, during those depression years, often chose plays that introduced the students to a world of gracious living that they could never have known in real life. Shy and awkward kids from the poorer parts of town became elegant ladies and gentlemen when they appeared in Mitchell's plays. They learned how to speak properly and how to choose the right fork for the salad and the right glass for white wine. Such attributes might have seemed trivial and irrelevant to their unemployed parents at the time, but for the students, it was good preparation for the life they would live when times got better. Drama was, as one student put it, "the only human course on the curriculum."

In 1942 the Rockefeller Foundation conducted a study on the state of amateur theatre in Canada. A Foundation representative came to Calgary to see a production of Thornton Wilder's *Our Town* presented at Western Canada High by Mitchell and her students. The representative was so impressed that he recommended a scholarship for the lead actor, Conrad Bain, and a two-year fellowship for Mitchell to study theatre at the college of her choice in the United States. Bain later went on to television stardom as a featured performer in such network shows as *Maude* and *Diff'rent Strokes*.

Mitchell completed a master of arts in theatre studies at the University of Iowa. She titled her thesis *An Amateur Looks at Professional Theatre*.

She returned to Calgary two years later to find that community theatre activity in the city had come to a full stop while she was away. The Theatre Guild had folded, leaving a vacuum that had yet to be filled. Western Canada High was still doing drama, but that was only for the students.

A group of her former students, eager to continue their studies in drama, provided the needed burst of new theatrical energy. Because the war was on, the group consisted mostly of women. Leading men were in short supply.

Through the school board, Mitchell organized night courses in costume and set design, makeup, voice projection, and other theatrical techniques. The wall between classrooms E14 and E15 at Western Canada High was demolished to provide space for classes and rehearsals. The students wanted to call themselves Workshop 15 after one of the two rooms where they studied and practised. Mitchell didn't like the name and changed it to Workshop 14. "Had more ring to it, you know."

Workshop 14 came close to becoming what Mitchell had always wanted in a theatre company. "Dear God, let me one day work with professionals," she had said. The Workshop 14 students wanted to become professional ("it was definitely not a little soda and snack group," said Mitchell) and many of them did. Alumni included such television actors as Bain and Chris Wiggins (*The Swiss Family Robinson*), set designer Jack McCullagh, and country singer Ray Griff.

Starting in 1946, Workshop 14 was a regular winner at the Alberta Drama Festival, capturing eleven provincial championships in thirteen years. "The ambition of every director in the province is to beat Betty Mitchell," said the president of the Alberta Drama League. "But to beat her, they're going to have to be good." Workshop 14 eventually stopped competing in the provincial festival to allow some of the other groups to win.

Workshop 14 also did well at the national level, winning nine major prizes in eleven years of competition at the Dominion Drama Festival. "We made ourselves thoroughly unpopular," said Mitchell.

By 1957, Workshop 14 was catering to anyone in Calgary with an interest in drama, not just Western Canada High graduates. That was the year Calgary and Edmonton both opened a twenty-seven-hundred-seat Jubilee Auditorium, built in celebration of the province's fiftieth birthday two years earlier. Workshop 14 finally had a place to play other than in a high school auditorium. For years, Mitchell had complained that a city without a real playhouse was like a "lifetime without dreams."

The Jubilee was a big place, but Workshop 14 had big dreams. The company opened the new auditorium with a production of John Patrick's *Teahouse of the August Moon*. The romantic lead was a young television announcer named Ed Whalen, who later achieved local success as Calgary's top sports broadcaster, and international fame as the drawling nasal voice of the much-syndicated, much-bootlegged *Stampede Wrestling* television programs.

Mitchell retired from teaching in 1961 and moved to Edmonton to guest lecture at the University of Alberta. She returned to Calgary in 1964 to find that, once again, things had fallen apart in her absence. Workshop 14 had declined, and other community groups had moved in to steal the limelight that once belonged to Mitchell and her charges.

Workshop 14 eventually merged with another amateur company, the Musicians and Actors Club Theatre Society, to form MAC 14, the nucleus of what became the professional Theatre Calgary in 1968. By then, Mitchell no longer occupied centre stage in local theatre. But her name, at least, was on the theatre in the Allied Arts Centre, the converted tractor warehouse where Theatre Calgary presented its plays. That last link was severed when Theatre Calgary moved to a new home in the Calgary Centre for Performing Arts in 1985. There, the spiritual descendants of Betty Mitchell have installed a bronze bust honouring the memory of the writer W.O. Mitchell (no relation) but have yet to pay similar tribute to the founding first lady of Calgary theatre. Only a small theatre in the basement of the Jubilee Auditorium bears her name.

In the last year of her life, Mitchell characterized herself as "just an old schoolmarm with theatre in my veins," and told her biographer, Kenneth Dyba, that she hated growing old, especially without children. "I'm a barren spinster," she said, "an antique." She had once contemplated marrying "my rancher beau, the chap from Brooks," but marriage would have meant "giving up my teaching and my theatre ways." Instead she opted for the theatre and a life without children.

Mitchell did have her theatrical children, and they carried on with what she had started. Today we don't wait around for the colonial governor to fill our halls with culture. We do it ourselves.

"Calgary would have been a barren place theatrically, if it had not been for Betty Mitchell," wrote journalist Andrew Snaddon after she died in September 1976 at age eighty. "Travelling theatre groups were pretty well non-existent in the thirties, forties, and early fifties. It was Betty Mitchell who took the high school play and made it much more than an exercise for precocious boys and girls facing an uncritical audience of daddies and mommies. She was, essentially, an outstanding teacher. She made a lasting contribution to all her students, and to her community."

Peggy Holmes
Canada's oldest broadcaster
1897–1997

Peggy Holmes was the quintessential little engine that could. Her pioneering experiences, as former Alberta premier Peter Lougheed noted in the introduction to one of her books, could "stimulate a whole wealth of memories of our early days as a province, and as a community of close networks and enduring friendships."

In her twenties, she homesteaded in the bush north of St. Paul, a First World War bride from England who didn't know the first thing about living in the Canadian wilderness. In her thirties and forties, she worked in Edmonton as a plumber, self-taught from her years on the farm. In her sixties, she took up painting. In her seventies, she became a writer. And at age seventy-seven, she became Canada's most unlikely rookie broadcaster.

Her late-blooming radio career happened in much the same way as the other ventures in her life. She didn't take any extensive training beforehand—she learned by doing. Peggy jokingly told people the letters of her degree were D.O.P.E.—Doctor of Personal Experiences.

The homesteading was typical. She came to Canada with her new husband, Harry, in 1918, settled in the Ashmont area northeast of Edmonton, and "with stars in our eyes and our feet firmly planted in the gumbo," cleared the land and built a two-storey log cabin. The couple didn't have time to finish the roof before the snow flew, so they pitched a tent in the living room to survive their first winter.

They left the farm after three years and moved to Edmonton, where Peggy worked as a bookkeeper and realtor before deciding she could make more money as a plumber. Harry worked as a provincial court reporter, a job he kept until he was eighty.

Peggy retired in her early sixties and took up painting as a hobby. "Being a true Albertan, my medium was oil," she quipped. She completed more than three hundred paintings, signing them Semloh (Holmes spelled backwards).

Her writing career came about as a result of a creative writing class she took at an Edmonton seniors' centre. Her instructor, the playwright Elsie Park Gowan, encouraged her not to worry about the technicalities of the craft. "Don't waste your time," Gowan advised. "Write about things you know."

Harry provided another kind of encouragement. "You're a rotten speller and you cannot punctuate for nuts," he said. "But keep on writing. You have a natural feel for a story and a lot of creative ability. After all, look at Churchill. He couldn't spell."

"Churchill had a full-time secretary," grumbled Peggy.

Harry then encouraged her to go one step further with her writing by taking it to the CBC. Peggy didn't know if the CBC would be interested, but she gathered up a sheaf of her stories about homesteading and drove to the radio station to find out. She was told the stories were too long for on-air purposes, but that they might have some radio potential if she could distill them into five-minute scripts.

Peggy had never heard of scripts before, but she went home and wrote some. When she returned, CBC staff put her in front of a microphone. She had never used one of those either. Producer Jackie Rollans listened to the audition, pronounced her "a natural," and offered Peggy a spot on the early morning radio show, five days a week.

"This Cinderella story is so unlikely, I still find it hard to believe," said Peggy. "Who could have foreseen that my timid inquiries would produce such dramatic results?"

She talked on the radio about her early life in Canada. "Homesteading in the twenties was tough," she told her audience. "But at the time, I didn't know any better. Nobody did." She told the story about pitching the tent in the living room and about feeding the chickens from her best Royal Doulton china.

Peggy soon ran out of homesteading stories, but the CBC, eager to keep her, suggested she write about anything that might be of interest to older people. Seniors were an untapped radio audience, she was told. Peggy broadened her scope and, whenever she ran out of ideas, she said she could "stick in a good murder" culled from Harry's court reporting days. She moved from the local morning show to broadcasting twice weekly on the CBC's Alberta regional network. She also co-hosted *Something for Seniors* on CKUA Radio.

Peggy wrote and broadcast more than one thousand scripts during her fifteen years in radio. She became known as the "oldest broadcaster in Canada" when fellow octogenarian Gordon Sinclair conceded during a Toronto broadcast that he was a year younger. "But he does have much more money," observed Peggy.

At age eighty-two, Peggy published her autobiography, *It Could Have Been Worse.* The title was a phrase her husband often used during their homesteading years. "The woods could be burning around us, and he would still say that things could be worse."

On her ninetieth birthday, the CBC arranged a surprise on-air party, with visiting celebrity pianist Marvin Hamlisch on hand to do the honours. "I guess the CBC must like what I do," said Peggy, "because they don't keep you on for the good of your health."

The end, when it came, was not pretty. At age ninety-two, Peggy was pulled off the air by the CBC. She announced her departure on her final broadcast for *Saturday Morning,* a program heard across Alberta, and said retirement was not her idea. One caller hailed her as a national treasure. "Sure," snorted Peggy, "a hidden treasure here at the CBC."

The *Saturday Morning* host suggested she might return for occasional guest appearances. "I don't think that will happen," retorted Peggy. "Face the facts. At my age, I've faced a lot of facts." She did agree with one caller, however, that the cancellation might lead to other career opportunities. "I always say that when one door closes, another opens." She still had no plans to retire.

Peggy published two more volumes of her memoirs and received numerous awards, including the Order of Canada and an honorary doctorate from the University of Alberta. She also had an Edmonton park named after her.

Peggy died in October 1997, a few weeks short of her one hundredth birthday. "They say you can't teach an old dog new tricks," she once said. "Well, I believe you can."

Stastia Cross Carry

Circus performer

1898–1995

Historians would have you believe that the Canadian West was never really "wild" like the American West; that it was won by negotiations and treaties, not by gunfights and killings. In fact, for a while there in the 1880s, Calgary did resemble a wild western town. It had illegal bars, open gambling and prostitution, and was briefly home to the famous outlaw Harry Longbaugh—also known as the Sundance Kid. Sitting Bull brought a touch of the real Wild West to southern Alberta when he fled north after the Battle of the Little Bighorn. Promoter Guy Weadick brought the showbiz version of the Wild West here when he started the Calgary Stampede. And Stastia Carry brought a trunkload of her own Wild West memories with her when she settled in southern Alberta during the 1920s.

Stastia Carry lived a fairy-tale life. For those who might doubt her, she had the pictures and the yellowed newspaper clippings to prove it. Her adventures began when she ran away from home at age sixteen to join a circus. She eventually became an accomplished trick rider and animal trainer, made a movie with Will Rogers, married a rodeo star named Alberta Jim, and lived to be ninety-seven.

Stastia carried her souvenirs, photos, and clippings in a big, black steamer trunk that came from New York and travelled with her all her life. But it didn't reveal all her secrets. It didn't say, for example, why she cut off contact with her family in California after she left home in 1914. Nor did it say what happened to the sequined costumes she wore when she toured with her husband in a Wild West show.

She was born to the showbiz life. Her father, Henry H. Cross, was an artist and adventurer who travelled the world painting western subjects and whose paintings now hang in Calgary's Glenbow Museum. Her mother, Nora Hauk, was a prominent vaudeville pianist and singer who lived with her children on a millionaire cousin's California ranch while her husband went travelling.

Postcards from her father showed young Stastia a world beyond the Santa Anita ranch where she grew up. One she always kept showed two mice being hypnotized by a cat. "Beware of the mouse trap," her father wrote. "There are traps set everywhere."

The card was dated 1914, the year Stastia followed in her father's itinerant footsteps and headed for Chicago. She joined the three-ring Sparks Circus as an elephant trainer and proved to be a natural for the job. With a glance of her eye and the slightest motion of her hand, it was said, she could control and bend to her will fifty tons of lumbering elephant.

Stastia worked for five different circuses both as an animal trainer and as a sharpshooter and trick rider. She also worked for the Wild West shows that travelled in tandem with circuses and vaudeville shows. Riding competitively, she won several trophies, including a West Coast championship in a Los Angeles rodeo that drew the attention of humourist Will Rogers. He invited Stastia to star opposite him in a movie, and she appeared in the 1920 silent flick *Cupid the Cowpuncher*.

Stastia met "Alberta Jim" Carry at a Wild West show in St. Louis in 1922. He was a skilled horseman and trick roper from Kew, near Millarville. After a two-day courtship, they married. Stastia joked afterwards that she fell in love with his horse first.

The couple spent the rest of the 1920s travelling the Wild West show circuit together. She wowed fans by hanging off the back of her horse at full gallop, while Jim drew applause for roping a dozen horses in full flight. They formed a company, A.J. Carry's Wild West Hippodrome Attractions, and took it on the road every summer. During the winter Jim worked on ranches around southern Alberta while Stastia sewed new costumes for their show. In 1927 they toured with a large group of Alberta cowboys, including Guy Weadick and Pete Knight, to promote the Calgary Stampede.

The road took its toll in terms of broken bones, sprains, and other injuries. It became increasingly difficult to attract audiences during the depression, and the growing popularity of movies and radio didn't help. A bad accident at a show in Guelph, Ontario—in which Stastia's elephants stampeded out of control, injuring her and killing a spectator—finally caused the Carrys to give up the performing life. They folded their tent, moved to the Peace River country, and put down roots as homesteaders. Jim first worked the horse-racing circuit as a trainer for area thoroughbred owners, then he and Stastia travelled with their own string of horses to tracks across the country.

They moved south to Black Diamond in 1943, where they managed a ranch and raised racehorses. Jim died in 1970. Stastia lived for another twenty-five years and became known around the area as a tough old biddy who played poker, told dirty jokes, and did all the things that people are not supposed to do if they want to live a long time. She smoked, drank Amaretto and milk cocktails, put sugar on her lettuce and vegetables, consumed candy and chocolates like they were going out of style, and ate everything that was fattening or sweet or both.

Stastia spent her final years at the High Country Lodge in Black Diamond. She decorated her room with purple violets, opened up her old steamer trunk, and regaled her friends with colourful stories about her life on the road. She died in September 1995. Three years later, her nieces opened up her trunk, sorted and catalogued the contents, took them to a Calgary art gallery, and put the memorabilia on display. "I was in awe of these pictures," said her niece Alleyne Wyler. "By reproducing some of them we have enhanced the history and what she was all about."

Carl Anderson
Farm crusader
1898–1998

Carl Anderson was an angry man when he and a group of fellow farmers formed a co-operative to take over a money-losing irrigation system built by the Canadian Pacific Railway near Brooks, east of Calgary.

Anderson was angry because he had been duped. He had come to Canada from Nebraska in 1918, lured by CPR advertising brochures promising mild winters and rich crops. Neither turned out to be true.

There were other betrayals. The CPR took almost ten years to build a promised spur line linking the irrigated farmland to the main line. The company refused to renegotiate land and irrigation contracts with struggling farmers. And it misled them about its operating losses when the farmers decided to take over the irrigation project.

Anderson had known he wasn't moving to an agricultural Eden when he and his father settled on a 220-acre property near Scandia, on the north bank of the Bow River, south of Brooks. The region was often called the Great American Desert because it was bereft of wells or natural ponds from which to draw needed water. But it did have the irrigation canals built by the CPR to divert water from the Bow, boost the crop-growing potential of the land, and attract homesteaders. The CPR had acquired the land from the Dominion government in return for building Canada's first transcontinental railway.

The Andersons might have settled in the Peace River country of northern Alberta, where there was prime farmland with natural moisture. But they were enticed by the CPR promotional literature offering land at fifty dollars an acre and promising forty bushels of wheat per acre that would sell for two dollars a bushel. They were told not to bring winter clothing because it rarely snowed. And if it did snow, the chinooks would quickly melt it.

Anderson was nineteen when he moved to Canada. Born in Omaha, he had dropped out of high school and was working on a ranch in northwestern Nebraska, serving his apprenticeship in livestock management, when he heard about the cheap farmland in southern Alberta.

In the spring of 1918, Carl and his father broke and seeded the first sixty acres of their new irrigation farm. They had tried to cultivate one hundred acres, but the land was so dry that the equipment kept breaking down. From those sixty acres, they took 720 bushels of fibre flax and—as promised by the CPR—earned a handsome return, amounting to $1,440.

It was a good start, but the euphoria was short-lived. The next winter was so cold that stock died and ranchers had to borrow money from the bank to buy feed.

Grain prices dropped steadily during the next decade. Wheat, which had sold for two dollars a bushel in 1918, was worth only thirty cents a bushel in 1930. Stock prices dropped as well. By 1933, the average farm income was less than $400 a year. The farmers' bitterness intensified when the CPR refused to meet their demands for a moratorium on land payments. Many of them abandoned their farms because the struggle was too much.

Eventually, with Anderson leading the way, the remaining farmers agreed to gamble everything on taking over the CPR's irrigation system. In 1935 they struck a deal to buy the system for $500,000, paid at $25,000 a year, interest-free. Then a government audit revealed the railway's losses were ten times higher than the company had reported. Anderson felt like a fool. He had worked hard to sell the farmers on the plan, and now it turned out that the company had pulled the wool over his eyes.

Facing failure, Anderson and his colleagues made another offer. They would take the money-losing irrigation system off the CPR's hands if the company paid them $400,000 to cover the operating losses of the next two years. The CPR counter-offered, and the two sides eventually agreed to settle for $300,000.

The farmer-owned Eastern Irrigation District began operations in 1935 and, within a short time, because of smart management, began to turn its losses around. The irrigation system made money, and the farmers made money. Anderson paid off his $10,550 mortgage in two years. Within sixteen years, all farmers in the district had free title to their land, one of Anderson's greatest satisfactions.

Anderson continued to work on behalf of his fellow farmers in the years that followed. He served as the first chairman of the EID board from 1935 until 1941. Between 1947 and 1964, he worked as the EID's general manager, helping farmers switch from grain production to more profitable livestock marketing through the use of feeder associations—co-operative purchasing groups.

In 1974, at age seventy-six, Anderson was elected to the Agricultural Hall of Fame. By then, he had mostly retired from farming, but he did continue to buy and sell cattle until well into his mideighties. When his wife Leila died in 1984, he established scholarships in her name and gave his volunteer time to the EID Historical Park Museum in Scandia. He had met Leila when she came from New Brunswick in the 1920s to teach in Scandia.

Anderson lived in Brooks until 1995 when, at age ninety-seven, he surrendered his driving licence, parked his Mercedes, and moved to the home of his niece Joyce Cann in Lethbridge. Life for him after that consisted of quietly looking after his affairs, visiting with friends, and cheering for the Toronto Blue Jays.

He turned one hundred in July 1998, and before he died the following November, he said he was no longer angry with the CPR. Oil had been found on EID grazing land in 1965, and the oil royalties that poured in at the rate of $4 million a year helped ease the bitterness.

Did Anderson ever have second thoughts about moving to this parched land, where farming was always a struggle? No, he said. People had once told him it was a mistake to try and farm on irrigated land but, in hindsight, he had no regrets.

Vera Jacques Ireland
Funeral home operator
1898–1999

Few expected Vera Jacques to succeed when her husband George died
suddenly in 1937, leaving her with a thirteen-year-old son to support.
She was, after all, a woman and a member of a generation that had
been told by their Victorian parents that there would never be a place
for women in the world of business. But Vera did succeed. She took
over the running of her husband's recently opened funeral home and,
in the words of the late *Calgary Herald* columnist Johnny Hopkins,
"made the doubters eat crow."

Vera's only previous business experience was as a secretary, but she
had always proven herself to be a quick study. She had started school
at age four, accompanying her six-year-old sister Lola to classes, and
had kept pace with her older sister until they finished high school
together. Vera was fourteen when she graduated.

Vera graduated from Garbutt Business College in Calgary in 1913,
then three years later, she landed an eighty-five-dollar-a-month job as
secretary to the western manager of Famous Players. That same year
she met and married George Jacques, a recent graduate of the New
York College of Embalming. She was eighteen, he was twenty-two.

The couple first settled southeast of Calgary in Vulcan, a town
which then had a population of 450. George ran the local funeral par-
lour, augmenting the family income by running a taxi service and
confectionery store.

Three months after moving to Vulcan, they lost everything in a
house fire and had to rebuild their home and business. They remained
in Vulcan for a few more years, then moved to Red Deer, and finally
back to Calgary, where their son, Murray, was born in 1924.

By 1930 George had saved enough money to open the first Jacques
Funeral Home in an old boarding house in the Victoria Park area, a
few blocks west of the Stampede grounds.

George eventually tore down the old boarding house and built a new Jacques Funeral Home—also known as the Little Chapel on the Corner—at the same location. Vera, by then, had learned a thing or two about the funeral business. She did the bookkeeping for her husband, played the organ at chapel services, and even tried her hand at embalming.

In 1937, just a few months after he opened his new building, George suddenly became seriously ill and died. Vera felt she had no alternative but to take over operation of the funeral home to support herself and her son. "True friends, generous creditors, and a loyal staff came to my aid," she said.

She advertised the business through a non-denominational radio program called *Chapel Chimes,* broadcast live from the Jacques Funeral Home over CFAC Radio. The program, which featured organ and vocal music, and readings of inspirational poems, ran on CFAC until 1964. The poems were anthologized in two popular booklets that could still be found in Calgary homes in the 1990s.

Murray Jacques graduated from the University of Alberta in 1947 and joined his mother as a business partner. Three years later Vera married chartered accountant Bill Ireland, a family friend who had served as auditor and financial adviser. Their marriage lasted thirty years, until Ireland's death.

In 1981, when Vera was eighty-three, she and Murray sold Jacques Funeral Home. Murray remained involved with the business, working with his sons Laurie and Douglas, while Vera took on a new role—as a volunteer driver for Meals on Wheels. She was the oldest driver on their roster. Every Wednesday, she climbed into her Oldsmobile and delivered lunches to a dozen people—all of them younger than she was—at inner-city locations.

Vera was still driving at age ninety-six. She received a two-year extension on her driver's licence and told a reporter she was very grateful to be able carry on. "I never think about being old," she said. "I just call myself chronologically enriched." She hoped she would have "enough sense" to stop driving if her health should break down and she were to become a danger to herself and others. "I don't want to encourage others to drive who shouldn't."

In 1995 Vera turned in her driver's licence and parked her Oldsmobile. She died in February 1999 at age one hundred. The

Jacques family continues to be associated with the funeral business in Calgary, though not with the funeral home that still bears their surname. Grandsons Laurie and Douglas Jacques run the Calgary Crematorium and the appropriately named Heritage Family Funeral Services, carrying on a family tradition that has spanned three generations and close to eighty-five years.

Charlie Edgar

Mountie and mayor

1901–1997

Charlie Edgar was one of Fort Macleod's most colourful citizens, an adventurous spirit who packed plenty of living into his ninety-five years. Among other things, he was a soldier, Mountie, farmer, actor, Boy Scout leader, rodeo cowboy, Kainai chieftain, plumber, amateur musician, and municipal politician.

He was also a good talker. He talked his way into the Canadian army as a boy bugler at age fifteen, hoping to see some cavalry action in Europe during the First World War. However, when the military authorities discovered he was too young for active service, they refused him permission to leave Alberta.

Still determined to go overseas, Edgar joined the Royal North-West Mounted Police, hoping to be sent to Russia as part of a special force raised to keep the peace between the White Russians and the Bolsheviks. That initiative took him only as far as Regina. The Allies withdrew before he had a chance to board ship.

Edgar had done his fair share of travelling before he joined the forces to see the world. Born in India, where his father was stationed with the King's Own Scottish Borderers, Edgar spent his early years living at his father's birthplace in Ireland, then lived in Scotland for a few years. At age nine he moved with his parents and siblings to the Fort Macleod area, where his father became a farmer after leaving soldiering behind.

Edgar's career with the Mounties lasted little more than two years. He broke horses in return for a splendid red serge uniform, one dollar a day, and all the food he could eat. "The grub made up for it," he said. But it wasn't exactly what he had had in mind when he signed up. As the only enlisted man at the post, he was expected to "do all the 'joe' jobs"—scrubbing floors, exercising the commander's mount, and doing whatever else needed doing.

He quit the Mounties when they refused to give him a raise of twenty-five cents a day and returned to Fort Macleod to work for the Canadian Pacific Railway. The railway paid him more than double his policeman's salary to stoke the boilers on the steam engines.

Looking back on his short-lived police career, Edgar said it was perhaps just as well that he never made it to Russia because the Mounties had no real role to play in the conflict beyond "getting shot at from both sides."

In 1923 he and two hundred other CPR workers lost their jobs when the railway moved its operations to Lethbridge. Edgar farmed with his father for a while and became an accomplished trick rider. The following year he starred in A. D. Kean's *Policing the Plains*, a silent movie about the Royal North-West Mounted Police. The movie, based on a true story, tells about a Peigan Indian who killed a mounted policeman during the late 1800s. Edgar played the ill-fated Mountie, Sergeant Wilde, and was required to fall from his horse four times for the sake of movie glory. Edgar also brought his riding skills to the Calgary Stampede, where he was one of the last men to board Midnight, the coal-black bronc regarded by rodeo historians as the greatest bucking horse in the history of the Stampede.

Edgar married an English-born immigrant named Margaret Elizabeth in 1925 and abandoned farming to apprentice as a plumber and sheet metal worker. He was soon working as foreman of the Fort Macleod waterworks department and earning an additional ten dollars per month as a night security guard at the local police lockup. In his spare time, he played the cornet in local bands, volunteered with the Boy Scouts, and cemented strong bonds with the local Native community.

Edgar travelled again during the Second World War, when he worked for both the Canadian and American governments, installing water systems in northern British Columbia and Alaska. But for all intents and purposes, he was now permanently settled in Fort Macleod with his wife, two sons, and a daughter.

Edgar established a plumbing business in Fort Macleod after the war, operating it with his two sons. His son Bill later went into the funeral business, moved to Olds, and became mayor of that community in 1969.

Edgar became mayor of Fort Macleod during his son's second

term of office in Olds. To avoid any hint of conflict of interest, he retired from the plumbing business when he was elected to Fort Macleod town council in 1970. Edgar served for sixteen years, six as mayor. A near-fatal car accident forced him to quit for one term, but he returned to serve until 1989, when he was eighty-eight years old.

His past experience with the Fort Macleod waterworks department served him in good stead during his years in municipal office. He was always able to plot the routes of the old water mains on a map whenever the question came up.

On his ninetieth birthday, in 1991, Fort Macleod named Charlie Edgar Street after the man they never called Charles, and granted him the freedom of the town. "I've been waiting for this since 1910," said the town's most beloved citizen, holding up the big key and recalling that he had lived in Fort Macleod for eighty-one years. Macleod Member of Parliament Ken Hughes commented that Charlie, through his RNWMP and CPR experiences, embodied the spirit of the pioneer settlers. "That's the kind of spirit that built western Canada," said Hughes, "the kind of spirit that built this whole country."

Edgar received other awards during his life, including an honorary chieftainship in the Blood tribe that acknowledged his long-time support for Native causes, and formal recognition for his volunteer work with Cubs and Scouts.

As Edgar aged through his nineties, his health and quality of life deteriorated. He had to surrender his driver's licence because of failing eyesight, and that broke his spirit. Whenever a reporter came to call, however, he invariably brightened up and marvelled at how lucky he was. "I didn't make a million dollars, but I've had a good life," he told one interviewer. "I just wish I could do it all over again." He died in Fort Macleod in April 1997 at age ninety-five.

Bert Sheppard
Cowboy
1901–1999

When 1998 was designated as the Year of the Cowboy in Alberta, a Toronto newspaper reported that the preferred transportation for the modern cowboy was the half-ton truck and that more than fifty thousand urban and rural cowboys in Alberta had bought such trucks in the previous twelve months. It seemed a far cry from the days when the cowboy was someone like Bert Sheppard, a man who spent most of his life on horseback, riding the ranges and the mountain passes with the smell of campfire and burning hides in his nostrils.

Sheppard fell in love with the cowboy life as a child and he remained a cowboy for all of his ninety-seven years. Two years before he died, he told a Calgary newspaper he was still a "working cowhand." He hadn't sat on a horse for years, but in his mind's eye he was twenty-one again, back in the saddle, riding the rangeland around the headwaters of the Highwood River, south of Calgary.

Born on his family's Cottonwood Ranch near the town of High River, Sheppard was the youngest and smallest son of a Northwest Territories justice of the peace and his wife, who had met on a ship while en route to Canada from Australia. Bert attended the original Calgary Stampede in 1912 when he was eleven, and he remembered it for the rest of his life. "It was quite a do," he recalled. "Those taking part were range cowboys. The horses they rode were the same ones that they rode ten to sixteen hours a day on the range."

Sheppard became a range cowboy himself in his teens. At age twenty-one, he went to work for the famed Bar U Ranch, which then boasted the world's largest herd of registered percheron horses—more than seven hundred. The ranch was owned by George Lane, one of the so-called Big Four backers of the 1912 Calgary Stampede.

He never became a rodeo cowboy, though he undoubtedly had the skills. Instead, he performed "mostly for an audience of coyotes."

All told, Sheppard tamed horses for about seventeen years, and he earned a reputation as one of the top bronc riders in the area. Even after leaving the Bar U, he continued to break horses for the ranch. "Although I was getting pretty well shook up from breaking horses, I stuck with it until I was spitting up blood," he said. Sheppard would ride up from his parents' ranch every Sunday and collect six wild broncs from the Bar U. The following weekend, he would ride back with all the horses broken. "Horse breaking consists of encouraging the horse to do the right things and discouraging him from doing the wrong," he said.

Sheppard finally gave up horse breaking when "my insides got churned," and he moved to the management side of the ranching business. He started breeding Herefords, choosing the breed because "they are better rustlers than other cattle. They will get out and rustle for food. And they have a thick, curly coat so they can stand the cold weather better."

In 1934 Sheppard bought the old Riverbend Ranch on the Highwood River near Longview, and later he assumed co-ownership, with three other ranchers, of the TL Ranch on Sullivan Creek. He also managed and became part owner of the OH Ranch, west of Longview. The OH dated back almost to the beginning of ranching in the Longview area. Established in 1883 by traders O. H. Smith and Lafayette French, it was renamed Rio Alto (Spanish for "high river") in 1900.

Sheppard retired to the Riverbend in 1963, but he continued to retain part of the Rio Alto. At the age of seventy he published a memoir of his life in ranching, called *Spitzee Days*. The title derived from *ispitsi,* the Native word for the tall cottonwood trees that grow along the Highwood River. "A gem among local histories," wrote a Calgary columnist. "Mr. Sheppard—who received his higher education from the back of a horse—writes for the general rather than the community audience."

Spitzee Days quickly sold out, and Sheppard followed it with another local history book, *Just About Nothing.* It too painted a colourful portrait of life on the range as it used to be, and it became a popular seller. The High River Historical Society characterized Sheppard as "a quiet, sensitive man who made a practice of observing, listening, and remembering."

Sheppard illustrated his books—and decorated his home—with the work of local western artists. He supported them, he said, because "they are natural artists who know something about cattle and horses."

In 1990 Parks Canada designated the old Bar U Ranch as a national historic site. Sheppard commissioned sculptor Rich Roenisch to create a $150,000, fifteen-foot bronze statue of George Lane, who had owned the Bar U from 1902 to 1927. "I made money out of my ranching experience," said Sheppard, "and I would like to honour Lane, the man who taught me the business."

The statue was based on the Charles M. Russell painting *George Lane Attacked by Wolves* and depicted an incident that occurred in 1886. Lane had been riding the range when he came upon a pack of wolves attacking one of his cows. He rode his horse into the pack, shot three of the wolves as they fled the scene, and picked off a fourth when it leaped up and fastened its jaws on his stirrup cover.

Sheppard spent several years trying to persuade Parks Canada to accept the Lane statue for the Bar U Ranch. The government initially rejected the gift as "not appropriate" and a "modern intrusion" on what was supposed to be a re-creation of a working ranch of the 1880s. A federal official said the statue would give too much prominence to Lane over the other Bar U owners, Fred Stimson and Pat Burns. Besides, the wolf incident had occurred on another ranch, not the Bar U. And there was some question as to whether it was wise to present a wolf-killing range rider as a representative of the cattle industry.

Parks Canada eventually changed its mind, after seven hundred High River area residents signed a petition urging the government to "accept this generous gift from a prominent member of our community."

The people of High River were very proud of Sheppard. In 1991, at a celebration of his ninetieth birthday, former Prime Minister Joe Clark called him a "national institution." Sheppard was still riding a horse at the time, and he attributed his longevity to both his bachelorhood and the healthy cowboy lifestyle. "I've cowboyed all my life and lived in the open air all the time," he said.

Sheppard died in February 1999, two weeks short of his ninety-eighth birthday. Sculptor Roenisch paid tribute: "I learned my cowboy ways from Bert. I rode a lot of miles with Bert. And we drank some whisky too. We had a lot of good times. We owe him a great hand of gratitude for the contribution he has made."

Catherine Barclay

Hostelling movement founder

1902–1985

Catherine Barclay and her sister Mary were the Lennon and McCartney of the hostelling movement in Canada. While each may have deserved individual recognition for particular contributions, the overall credit was always jointly shared. The Calgary Jaycees acknowledged this in 1973 when they chose their annual Citizen of the Year. They prepared two citations and two awards because their "citizen" was the two Barclays.

Both sisters were teachers. Mary, older by one year, trained at the University of Toronto and the University of Chicago and spent much of the time in her Calgary classroom fostering a love of nature among her students. Catherine travelled further afield to study at Columbia University in New York and at the Sorbonne in Paris, and she promoted in her classroom the finishing school attributes of properly written English, effective public speaking, and—forty years before the establishment of official bilingualism in Canada—fluency in French.

Catherine taught Grade nine at what is now Colonel Walker Community School in the Inglewood district of Calgary. A former student remembered her as a teacher who could be charming and witty when she wanted "but could also turn a class of fourteen-year-olds to stone with a withering glance."

Catherine believed in teaching French as a living language, and she was one of the first teachers in the city to promote student exchanges between Calgary and France. She believed the best way to attain fluency was to spend time in the country where the language was spoken. She also believed that young people should be able to travel to other countries without having to worry about the cost of accommodation.

In 1931 Catherine returned from a trip to Europe and told her sister Mary about the youth hostels she had seen abroad that made it possible for young travellers to spend time in places they might not otherwise afford. She wondered why Canada couldn't have something similar. "More people could enjoy the charms of the Rockies," she reasoned, "if they were able to stay in cheap lodgings."

Mary readily agreed, and two summers later, the sisters opened North America's first youth hostel in a farmer's field in Bragg Creek, in a tent rented for nine dollars from Calgary Tent and Awning. For twenty-five cents a night, hikers could buy protection from the elements and spartan comfort. The hostellers brought their own bedding and slept on straw ticks.

Back in her classroom, Catherine combined her passion for camping with her passion for French, and her students responded enthusiastically. During the fall and winter, they spent their Saturday afternoons converting raw wool into comforters. As soon as the winter snows started to melt, they set off for another season of hiking and hostelling in the mountains.

The Bragg Creek hostel achieved permanent status in 1935, when it upgraded from canvas to wood. The Barclay sisters joined forces with other hiking enthusiasts to form a group—initially all-female—called Canadian Youth Hostels, and the movement began to spread. New overnight stops were established for hikers travelling the trails from Bragg Creek to Banff and beyond. Catherine became the first president of the hostelling organization.

By the start of the Second World War, Calgary's enterprising sisters had established hostels in Ontario and Quebec and planned more for British Columbia and Atlantic Canada. At that point, Catherine began to gradually pull back from the movement to spend more time promoting French language and culture. She directed plays in French, organized a social group in Calgary for French speakers, and founded the French program at the Banff School of Fine Arts.

Mary became the chief spokesperson for the Canadian hostelling movement as Catherine focused more on her French-language projects. People began to consider Mary the founder of the movement, but she was always careful to credit her sister for having the passion and the organizational drive to make it a success.

Catherine remained a hiking and outdoors enthusiast until she died in 1985 at age eighty-three. Two years later, Mary Barclay received the highest tribute a Canadian can earn—investiture into the Order of Canada. That honour came too late for Catherine to share the glory, but the citation did acknowledge her contribution as cofounder. Later in 1987, local hostellers gathered near the original Bragg Creek site to unveil a commemorative marker dedicated to the two sisters. From a shaky beginning with a horse, two cars, and a rented tent, they had established the basis for a national network of more than seventy hostels that now serve thousands of Canadians and visitors from around the world.

Grant MacEwan

Farmer, teacher, politician, and writer

1902–2000

No book about the people who built Alberta would be complete without a chapter on Grant MacEwan. Farmer, academic, politician, and one of the province's most prolific social historians, MacEwan embodied quite a bit of history in himself. "Loaned for a season to our region," to use his own phrase, MacEwan worked tirelessly and enthusiastically for his adopted province until his own "season" ran out in June 2000.

Before leaving his mark in Alberta as a politician, environmentalist, and historian of western Canada, he distinguished himself in Manitoba and Saskatchewan as an agricultural scientist, professor, and university administrator.

MacEwan was born on a homestead near Brandon, Manitoba, where he learned early to make the best of difficult circumstances. He had to postpone going to high school, for example, when his father went broke manufacturing fire extinguishers. The younger MacEwan took time out to help his father re-establish as a farmer in Saskatchewan. But once he made it to university, there was no stopping him. Starting at age nineteen, he worked his way up to a master's degree in science, became a professor in animal husbandry at the University of Saskatchewan, and began a love affair with western history that would last to the end of his life.

In 1942 MacEwan began a broadcast series for CBC Radio about notable pioneers of the Canadian West. The series eventually evolved into *Sodbusters*, the first of more than fifty books he would write during the next fifty years. He wrote about horses and trains and farm life, and told the life stories of Pat Burns, John Ware, Bob Edwards, and dozens of other heroes and heroines of the Old West.

He wrote from a local perspective for a regional readership. "He is a truly western Canadian writer," wrote his biographer, Rusty Macdonald. "When he writes, he does not look over his shoulder toward eastern Canadian publishers, critics, reviewers. Nor does he look toward New York and Hollywood, or seek to impress colleagues as many other 'western' writers do."

In 1946 the University of Manitoba appointed MacEwan dean of the agriculture faculty. He became active in politics as a Liberal, quit his university job, and ran unsuccessfully in a federal by-election in Brandon in 1951.

He moved to Calgary the following year and one year later was elected to city council as an alderman. By now he was a full-time writer and politician. He served four terms as alderman and became mayor of Calgary for one term starting in 1963. At that point, MacEwan revealed the philosophy of "waste not, want not" that governed his life by asking that the mayor's salary of $13,500 a year be cut to $10,000. "We are too generous with our mayors," he declared. "The salary shouldn't be so high that it overshadows the service." Council rejected his proposal.

His Scottish Presbyterian mother had taught him, he said, that thrift was a virtue and waste a sin. He would stay at the YMCA, rather than at hotels, even after he became prominent in provincial politics. "The sheets are clean," he would tell his grumbling aides. "And the roof doesn't leak." Elected a member of the legislative assembly in 1955, MacEwan became Alberta Liberal leader in 1958. He lost the election the following year and resigned the leadership in 1960.

Though committed to Liberal causes, MacEwan was never comfortable with Liberal party discipline. In his later years he was drawn more to a politician's personal style than to party policy. He bought a membership in the Reform Party to support Preston Manning, the son of his former Social Credit opponent, Ernest Manning. "I like young Manning," said MacEwan. "I like his humility. By thunder, I think he's honest." But, MacEwan warned other Reformers, "don't expect me to be a campaigner."

MacEwan left partisan politics in 1965 to become Alberta's lieutenant governor for nine years. He insisted on doing the vice-regal job without the usual pomp and circumstance, claiming the right to preserve his simple lifestyle. He allowed no liquor to be served at official banquets. He continued to rise early for jogging, ate only porridge for breakfast, and refused to ride in the back seat of the official limousine.

"I like the front," MacEwan told his chauffeur, Henry Weber. "One is less conspicuous, and it's more congenial."

On one occasion, he asked Weber to stop the vice-regal car so he could help two teenagers push a van out of a ditch. On warmer days, he dispensed with the car entirely, opting to walk instead. Throughout his life MacEwan was a champion of walking and public transportation. He would take the bus rather than drive his car, and walk rather than take the bus.

Along with his fifty-six books, MacEwan generated more than three thousand newspaper columns, more than five thousand speeches, and one thousand broadcasts, plus countless magazine articles and contributions to scholarly, technical, and popular publications. His goal, he said, was to provide "entertaining, academic, and cultural values."

In 1967 the University of Calgary awarded him an honorary doctorate. In his convocation address, MacEwan talked about the naturalist religion that had evolved from his early Presbyterian faith. It promoted living in harmony with the natural environment and with all other living creations of God. He had built a log cabin from recycled telephone poles on his acreage south of Calgary so he wouldn't have to cut down living trees. In his mid-fifties, he had embraced vegetarianism. It was, wrote biographer Macdonald, "a space-age step for a man who had spent a good part of his life instructing in the proper raising of livestock for slaughter."

He lived by his own creed: "I am prepared to stand before my Maker, the Ruler of the entire Universe, with no other plea than that I have tried to leave things in His Vineyard better than I found them." Five universities awarded him honorary doctorate degrees. The federal government made him an officer of the Order of Canada. The Calgary Fire Department made him an honorary fire chief.

MacEwan earned more money than he could ever spend, so he gave most of it to the charitable Calgary Foundation, which set up two trusts for him—the $500,000 MacEwan Family Charitable Fund and the $100,000 Grant MacEwan Nature Protection Fund. "I lost my ambition to make a million dollars," he said. "I thought I was making a mistake letting my money pile up."

When he was ninety-one, MacEwan published a book on prairie humour. He continued to write until he was ninety-four, when an accident curbed his activities. After he fell in the bathroom of his apartment and broke two ribs, his family moved him to a nursing home in Calgary. He died there, in June 2000, two months short of his ninety-eighth birthday.

MacEwan's legacy to Alberta lives on in Calgary and Edmonton. At Calgary city hall, the MacEwan Library features a display of his books, some of which he kept in his office when he was mayor. In Edmonton, MacEwan Community College is named in recognition of his lifelong dedication to education.

The MacEwan Student Centre at the University of Calgary is named for his efforts—while mayor of Calgary—to establish the university as an autonomous institution, separate from the University of Alberta. The Calgary Board of Education named Grant MacEwan Elementary School in his honour. In northwest Calgary, the entire neighbourhood of MacEwan Glen evokes his memory. More than two dozen streets bear his name.

Wilf Carter

Country singer

1901–1996

Wilf Carter was the first country music star to come out of Alberta, a successful performer who paved the way for such later stars as Ian Tyson, k. d. lang, George Fox, and Paul Brandt. He was, as the song says, country before country was cool. Carter, in fact, was country before country was even country. In his day, it was called cowboy music.

He was born in Nova Scotia, one of nine children of a poor Baptist minister, and became an Albertan in his early twenties. He rode the rails westward to make his living as a ranch hand, and made his home in a deserted shack near Carbon with a mongrel dog for company. He skinned coyotes to supplement the "living money" he earned on the ranches, and spent much of his spare time composing songs and practising the cowboy yodel that would become his trademark. At age ten, he had paid twenty-five cents to attend a Chautauqua tent show, where he was inspired by a performer known as "The Yodelling Fool."

Carter's yodelling was distinctive—a "three in one" or "echo" yodel that few could emulate. "He had a sound," said country singer Ian Tyson, "that high, echoed sound that seemed to be bouncing off some Rocky Mountain glacier."

In 1929 Carter auditioned as a singer for Calgary radio station CFAC. When station management said he was not ready yet and suggested he come back in a year, Carter took the rejection in stride. He worked on his singing, performing at area dances and house parties, and in 1930 he tried again. Carter auditioned for another Calgary radio station, CFCN, which hired him to sing on a popular Friday night show, *The Old Timers*. He earned five dollars a show.

Mail began to pour into CFCN from all over the Prairies. Carter's growing popularity resulted in an invitation to entertain on the Canadian Pacific Railway's trail rides through the Rockies.

In 1933 he performed on the maiden voyage of the CPR's *SS Empress of Britain*. He stopped off en route to audition for RCA Records in Montreal, and recorded an original composition about the capture of Albert Johnson, the Mad Trapper. By the time he returned from the cruise, RCA had already pressed and released the recording. It became a best seller. On the flip side of the seventy-eight was a Carter yodelling tune called *Swiss Moonlight Lullaby*.

From there, Carter travelled to New York, where he auditioned for CBS Radio. After fifteen minutes of singing and yodelling, he was offered a contract to broadcast his own radio show. A CBS secretary typed out his song list and asked, "What name do I put on it?" "Any one will do," replied Carter. The young woman thought for a moment and typed "Montana Slim." Announcer Bert Parks of "Here she comes, Miss America" fame used the name to introduce Carter on his debut show for CBS. Carter liked the sound of the name and kept it. "Cowboys in my day always had nicknames," he said.

By 1934 Carter had become a star on CBS with a daily radio show that was broadcast over a national network of 250 stations. He received ten thousand fan letters a week.

But he missed the West, and in 1937 Carter moved back to Calgary and bought a 320-acre cattle ranch near what is now the Spruce Meadows showjumping facility. His new bride, a New York nurse named Bobbie Bryan, came with him.

Carter suffered a back injury in a 1940 car accident that took him away from performing for nine years. But because he had made so many records before the accident, the record company could keep releasing new songs as if he were still active. He returned to touring in 1949, and the following year set an attendance record at Toronto's Canadian National Exhibition, performing for fifty thousand people in one week.

In 1953, with his daughters Sheila and Carol performing as backup singers and dancers, Carter toured as "The Family Show With the Folks You Know." He made his first appearance on the grandstand stage at the Calgary Stampede nine years later. He had appeared as a cowboy at the Stampede during the 1930s and won money in the cow milking competition, but this was his debut appearance as a singer. Stampede organizers presented him with a trophy, honouring him as the "Balladeer of the Golden West, in sincere appreciation of thirty-three wonderful years."

Carter remained one of country music's most popular entertainers through the 1960s, and he continued to tour steadily through the 1970s and 1980s, when he was well into his seventies. As he grew older, he cut his performances back to twenty a year, but he continued to record, and he kept coming back to Calgary. From May to September, he lived on his farm near Spruce Meadows. "Calgary is my home, and the fans here are the best I've ever met," he said. He spent the rest of the year in Florida.

In 1972 RCA Records presented Carter with a plaque for his accumulated record sales. Country singer Tommy Hunter noted that Carter's first hit record, *The Capture of Albert Johnson,* had helped save RCA Records from bankruptcy during the depression. Other popular Carter tunes of the period had included *There's a Love Knot in My Lariat, There's a Bluebird on My Windowsill,* and *When It's Springtime in the Rockies.*

His honours included a place in the Songwriters' Hall of Fame in Nashville and the Martin Guitar Entertainer of the Year Award for his contributions to Canadian country music. Carter was blasé about the kudos. "They can give you all the awards in the world; that isn't what counts," he said. "It's the people. They've given me what I have today."

Carter recorded his last album, *Whatever Happened to All Those Years,* in 1988, when he was eighty-four, and he continued touring for another four years. "The only reason he quit, frankly, was because of his hearing," said Tommy Hunter.

Carter eventually sold his Calgary farm, but he kept an apartment in the city until a few years before his death. Even in old age, he continued to saddle up his horse Blaze and ride the range to work with cattle.

Carter died at his home in Scottsdale, Arizona, at age ninety-one, two months after being diagnosed with a stomach tumour. "He was the sound of western Canada in the 1930s and 1940s," said Ian Tyson. "You could not overstate his influence. He was the sound of Canada."

George DuPre

Hoaxer

1905–1971 (circa)

George DuPre earned his fifteen minutes of fame with a remarkable, if dubious, achievement. He deceived millions—including a distinguished war correspondent and the editors of *Reader's Digest* and Random House publishers—with a completely bogus account of his exploits as a secret agent during the Second World War.

"Charlatan," "impostor," "pathological liar"—all of these terms apply to this charming spinner of tall tales who found in Alberta a place where he could pass himself off as a war hero, a place where he could turn his back on the mundane reality of his actual wartime experiences and concoct a fantastic fiction about working as a spy in occupied France.

DuPre began his campaign of deception in Winnipeg when he came home from the war in the uniform of an RCAF flight lieutenant. His wife, Muriel, whom he had married in 1935, was shocked to discover he had aged almost beyond recognition and that his hair had turned prematurely white. He told her he had spent the war, not based at various RAF stations across England—as indicated in the fifty-five letters he had written home during the previous five years—but working with the French resistance movement as a spy, masquerading as a half-witted garage mechanic named Pierre Touchette.

DuPre continued the deception when the couple moved to Alberta in the late 1940s. He told his lies to service clubs and church groups in Edmonton, where he worked as assistant to provincial mines minister Nathan Tanner, and in Calgary, where he served as branch manager for Commercial Chemicals Ltd. Everywhere he went, he told audiences he had survived his war experiences because of his trust in God.

In 1953 an American war correspondent, Quentin Reynolds, heard about a luncheon speech DuPre had given to a group of Toronto businessmen and flew up from New York to interview him.

By that time DuPre was a respected member of the Calgary community. He volunteered with the Boy Scouts, taught Sunday school, and always attended the monthly meetings of the Canukeena Club, a group of ex-servicemen.

Reynolds had impeccable credentials as a war correspondent. He wrote the book *Dress Rehearsal*, which many consider the standard work on the ill-fated raid on Dieppe. When he said he found DuPre's story entirely credible, that was good enough for Random House and *Reader's Digest*. Both undertook to publish the story.

The 214-page Random House book about the "gentle spy who suffered the most gruesome tortures imaginable" appeared in October 1953. The *Reader's Digest* abridgement appeared the following month. Both were titled *The Man Who Wouldn't Talk*. The title was ironic since DuPre's problem was that he talked too much.

The story, as he told it, was that he was born George Cyril DuPre in 1906 in Poona, India, where his father was a colonel with the Royal Artillery. George was educated in England, graduated from Cambridge University with an arts degree, then moved to Canada. He worked with the Hudson's Bay Company for thirteen years, first transporting merchandise by dogsled in the western Arctic, then managing a muskrat ranch in Manitoba.

He said he had volunteered for the RCAF in Victoria in 1939 and was sent for intelligence training in England at a baronial mansion improbably named the Oxford Home for Convalescents. The following year he was parachuted into occupied France.

DuPre claimed he had worked in France for four years, organizing escape routes for downed British and American airmen. He was arrested by the Gestapo, questioned about his underground activities, tortured for several weeks, then released. He went back to working for the resistance, remained in France until 1944, then was posted to London before returning to Canada in December 1945.

Some of his story was factually accurate. DuPre had, in fact, volunteered for the RCAF and, because at age thirty-six he was considered too old for combat duty, he had spent his wartime service at air force stations in Canada and Britain. His work in Britain involved, among other things, debriefing fliers who had returned after landing in enemy territory.

DuPre's story began to unravel shortly after the Random House book and *Reader's Digest* article appeared. A former RCAF officer, producing a date-stamped photograph as proof, told a *Calgary Herald* reporter named Doug Collins that he and DuPre had been stationed together at an airfield in Victoria in 1942, two years after DuPre had supposedly been dropped into France.

Collins checked into DuPre's claims and found most of them to be false. He had never been in France during the war and had never worked in intelligence—though he had taken some intelligence training—and, needless to say, the Gestapo had never tortured him.

Collins confronted DuPre with his findings, and the impostor admitted that the story was a hoax. The *Herald* published the exposé under the headline "Calgarian Admits Secret Service Story Was Fabrication." DuPre lamely defended his lies, saying his only intent was to spread the message that survival depends on faith in God. He might have made up the facts, he said, but the message was pure truth.

News of the hoax created widespread consternation in Canada and the United States. Author Reynolds said he was "shocked and appalled" by the duplicity. *Reader's Digest* staff expressed surprise and said DuPre's "sincerity, integrity, and modesty" had impressed them. Random House relabelled the book as fiction and offered to refund the purchase price to disappointed customers. Most chose not to take advantage of the offer.

Reynolds was never able to explain satisfactorily how he could have been duped, and his reputation suffered lasting damage. Collins, meanwhile, went on to achieve recognition across Canada as a newspaper columnist and television journalist, but he damaged his own reputation in the 1990s when he became the first journalist in this country to face a human rights complaint over comments he made about Jews.

As for DuPre, he disappeared into obscurity after what the *Herald* called the "greatest hoax in the history of journalism." He continued to live and work in Calgary for another seventeen years before retiring and moving to Victoria with his wife and son in 1970. He died there some time later.

How did he get away with the hoax for so long? Partly because of the traditional official secrecy surrounding anything to do with intelligence work. In the beginning DuPre took a chance by telling his lies because there were plenty of people around who would have known the true details of his wartime service. However, the passage of time and the fading of memories, coupled with the fact that military authorities would never publicly refute his claims, allowed DuPre to promote his fabrications without fear of contradiction. In the absence of denial, the hoaxer flourished.

Hazel Braithwaite

Advocate for farm women

1905–1994

"Here come the farmers," was the rallying cry in provincial politics after the First World War, when the United Farmers of Alberta rose to power. And right behind them came the women.

The women were never quite as politically active as the men. For one thing, they didn't have their own elected provincial government party. But their voices were not silent. In 1915 they formed the United Farm Women of Alberta to campaign for women's suffrage, and one year later they won the right to vote.

Hazel Braithwaite joined their ranks ten years after women achieved the franchise. She was a twenty-one-year-old farm wife from the Red Deer area. She had moved to Alberta with her parents at age five and married farmer Clifford Braithwaite at age sixteen.

The story goes that Hazel was trying to exercise her newly acquired voting rights during the 1926 federal election when a crowd of men blocked her path. She couldn't be stopped then, just as she couldn't be stopped in the years following, when her career as a polit-ical activist took flight.

Words like "feminism," "affirmative action," and "gender equity" hadn't yet entered the household vocabulary when Hazel began working for the United Farm Women of Alberta. She just knew that she wanted to see change and help people. Women should be con-cerned with the outcome of the farming business, she said.

During her more than forty years of involvement with the UFWA, Hazel held every executive position in the organization, including that of president. Her concerns, she said, were anything that affected the farm family.

One concern was education. During her five years as UFWA pres-ident, Hazel frequently asked universities to relax their entrance requirements so that post-secondary education would become avail-able to a greater number of high school students.

She helped her own children through community college and university by working outside the home. During the Second World War, with men overseas serving their country, Hazel learned to operate various kinds of farm machinery to help relieve a provincial labour shortage. At the same time, she worked for the Red Cross and became the first director of civil defence for Red Deer West.

Hazel's interest in education brought her an affiliation with the Alberta Education Council, an appointment to the University of Alberta's board of governors, and election to the University of Alberta senate, which gave her another perspective on Alberta's educational system.

Newspapers characterized her as an outspoken firebrand. Typical of her blunt style was a comment she made after seventy-one-year-old Georges Vanier was installed as governor-general in 1959. The man is too old, declared Hazel. Canada needed a younger person for this job. Who would she suggest as an alternative? Hazel's candidate of choice was Lester Pearson.

A person can't belong to too many organizations, she once said, and causes from every social field seemed to find her. At different points in her career, Hazel served as a director of the John Howard Society, director of the Indian-Eskimo Association, a member of the Children and Family Welfare Council, and a member of the Red Deer and District Council on Aging.

While she was always active outside the home, Hazel said she believed it was as a mother and farm wife that she made her most important contributions. She raised six children on the farm, and their needs came before all others. When she died, her son John chronicled her various activist and political involvements, then added that his mother also cooked the best chicken and baked the best apple pie that anybody ever tasted.

One of her political involvements was with the New Democratic Party. She made a failed bid for a federal seat in 1965 after announcing her candidacy in typical style: "The rudderless ship of state" had floundered so badly, she said, that the whole institution of democratic government was losing the respect of the common people.

Hazel was inducted into the Alberta Agricultural Hall of Fame in 1978 and was praised for having promoted recognition of women as equal partners on the farm. She noted that while farm women had more control over the disposal of matrimonial property than in the past, their situation was still far from ideal. Just three years earlier the Supreme Court had ruled, in the Irene Murdoch case, that a Turner Valley woman who helped run the family ranch had done "just about what the ordinary rancher's wife does" and had no right to a share in it. The ensuing protest produced reforms in provincial matrimonial property laws across Canada.

Hazel and her husband moved to Sylvan Lake when they retired from farming. Hazel ran the Uptown Cafe and Movie Theatre and found new causes to promote. She served as manager of the Burnt Lake Historical Society, became active in the Women's Institute and Friendship Centre of Sylvan Lake, and drove a vehicle for the Meals on Wheels program.

After her husband died, Hazel moved back to Red Deer, where the interests of farm women occupied her to the end. She founded the Irene Parlby scholarship, named for the farm woman who became Alberta's first female cabinet minister. Parlby also participated, as one of the Famous Five, in the Persons case, which resulted in Canadian women being granted the right to run for public office.

Hazel funded the Parlby scholarship herself, through raffles and sales of her needlework. The scholarship, awarded annually to students attending agricultural college in Alberta, was her last significant contribution to the development of the farm industry in this province. She died in Red Deer in September 1994 at age eighty-nine.

Mary Dover

*Army officer, alderman, and
heritage preservationist*

1905–1994

Mary Dover was born on the day Alberta became a province, 1 July 1905, and throughout her long life she remained a living link with the province's pioneering past. Her grandfather was James F. Macleod, the man who led 275 officers and troopers of the North-West Mounted Police west from Winnipeg to what would become Calgary. Her father was A.E. Cross, one of the so-called Big Four who founded the Calgary Stampede. Mary didn't need a historian to tell her about Calgary's frontier beginnings. All she had to do was remember the stories she had heard at her father's knee.

Because she was a member of one of southern Alberta's leading families, it was easy for Mary Cross to fall into an idle lifestyle. As a young and single miss, she danced and partied with the most eligible young men of Calgary. At age twenty-one she was a stunt rider for actress Barbara Kent in the western movie *His Destiny*, filmed near Calgary. In 1927 she was named Queen of the Banff Winter Carnival. Three years later, she was travelling the Far East as the twenty-four-year-old bride of Melville Grant Dover, a dashing First World War flyer turned auto executive.

But there was more to Mary Dover than her privileged life of gay abandon would suggest. She had her opportunity to show that with the coming of the Second World War, when her husband became a major in the Ceylon Garrison Artillery, and Dover found herself back in Canada with her son, David. She joined the Canadian Women's Army Corps and assumed responsibility for interviewing prospective enlistees. She explained her involvement by saying, "There was a war on, and I didn't want to sit and knit."

The Canadian Women's Army Corps was a national amalgamation of the provincial volunteer women's service units that started forming in 1938, motivated by the belief that female soldiers should be able to take over non-combat duties from men dispatched to the front lines.

The women trained under the auspices of the Canadian army. In Calgary, Alberta corps members paraded on Wednesday nights at Western Canada High School and learned military drill, bookkeeping, first aid, and commissariat work. They also studied motor vehicle maintenance at Maclin Ford.

The CWAC was formed initially as a support unit for the active service force, but by March 1942, its status had been upgraded to that of an independent militia corps, subject to the same military regulations as the men. "It's not a women's organization," Dover stressed. "It is simply another corps in the army. Its members have a heavy responsibility."

She joined the corps as a staff officer for the Calgary district. "It was a time of crisis for everyone," she said. "I was doing anything I could." She rose quickly through the ranks and served in England during the Blitz. After that, she held the rank of lieutenant colonel, the second highest in the corps, commanding the CWAC training base in Kitchener, Ontario.

Dover was in Kitchener the day the D-Day troops landed in Normandy. Her first thought was that the women should do something. Many had husbands in France who were taking part in the invasion, and the women felt they should show some kind of solidarity. "So we decided on a parade through the town," said Dover. "We didn't have a band, but we did have drummers." Four companies of women and a small platoon of men, mostly veterans of the First World War, took part in the parade. It started just as the citizens of Kitchener were heading for work and school. "They heard the drums, and the effect was incredible," said Dover. "People just seemed to erupt out of their houses. We actually caused a traffic jam as we headed to the war memorial right in the centre of town."

Wars, said Dover, have a tendency to "break things." Dredging up the details of war could sometimes seem unnecessary, and often perhaps even cruel, she said. But she had been born to parents who told their children that their country owed them nothing—that they, in fact, owed something to the country—and that was why she had signed up for the CWAC. "Our women release the men who hold the guns in their hands," she said. "The women of our enemies are fighting, and we have to fight them."

For her wartime service, Lt. Col. Dover received the Order of the British Empire. Though she joked about OBE standing for "old boiled eggs" (CBE: cold boiled eggs; MBE: many boiled eggs), she was proud of the honour. Her Victorian father had told her that while there would never be a place for her in the business world, "one should be useful." Serving one's country was about as useful as one could be.

After the war, Dover and her husband quietly separated, and she remained active for some years in a number of service organizations, particularly the Ex-Service Women's Club and the Canadian Legion. She eventually cut her formal ties with the armed services but maintained a fond connection with the "old boys" of the Colonel Belcher Veterans' Hospital. "They call me up and say, 'We're coming out,'" she told a Calgary newspaper in 1976, a dozen years after she started inviting the old soldiers to her country garden home near Millarville. They came by the busload and she served them "tea"—the kind her father used to sell after he established the first brewery in Calgary.

With her wartime service behind her, Dover's name became associated with peacetime service endeavours. She served two terms as city alderman, 1949–51 and 1957–60, and worked hard to preserve historic buildings and green spaces. She also ran twice, unsuccessfully, for the provincial Liberals. She volunteered for the Red Cross and the Women's Canadian Club, and served as Colonel in Chief of the Steele's Scouts, a band of make-believe soldiers who re-create major events in western history. Her involvement with this group had a serious intent, she said, because she wanted to promote public interest in western heritage.

She eventually tired of being interviewed about her own heritage and her role as a pioneering grande dame of early southern Alberta. But she never tired of recalling her association with the hundreds of young Canadian women who had served with her in the Canadian Women's Army Corps.

"We were unique," she said in 1991 during a fiftieth-anniversary reunion of the CWAC in Calgary. "It's a matter of great pride for the women."

Dover spent her last years gardening at the acreage home that she had named Oksi Hill, from the Blackfoot word for "all is well." "Life should be a vigorous affair," she said. "It shouldn't be something that tapers off and disappears."

She died in June 1994, three weeks short of her eighty-ninth birthday. "The leading families created a sense of belonging to Alberta," said historian Max Foran, "and as Alberta grew up, Mary carried on that tradition."

James H. Gray
Social historian
1906–1998

Jimmy Gray was our best chronicler of the manners and mores of the Prairies, which is to say he knew more about boozing and whoring between the Rockies and the Pas than any social studies expert around.

He was also a brave and principled man. When he quit a good job as Ottawa correspondent for the *Winnipeg Free Press* in 1948, it was because he disagreed with the paper's editorial stand on Canadian trade policy. For Gray, a pay cheque was not enough. The job also had to grant him dignity and autonomy. He would be an anomaly in today's workplace.

Gray wrote the first draft of his first book, *The Winter Years*, during the unhappy year he spent working in the Ottawa press gallery. That book, which failed to find a publisher for twenty years, set the tone and the style for all the books Gray wrote about the history of the Canadian West.

He had the great advantage, as a social historian, of being on hand for much of the action. "I am a little bit of everyone I have ever met," he said, and he wrote accordingly. He saw the First World War years and the 1919 Winnipeg General Strike through the eyes of a poverty-stricken youngster who sold newspapers and block ice and stood in line for food vouchers. His father's alcoholism meant a life of deprivation for the family, and Gray learned early to live by his wits.

He quit school after finishing Grade nine, landed a job as office boy at the Winnipeg Grain Exchange, and worked his way up to bookkeeper and stockbroker's clerk. During the depression, he lost his job, spent five months in a tuberculosis sanatorium, and then lived on relief, with his wife, Kathleen, and baby daughter, Patricia, in a cheap boarding-house.

The Winter Years tells that story. It tells not only about the impact of the depression on the farmers and city workers of the Prairies, but about the struggle of a twenty-five-year-old husband and father searching desperately for work after the stock market crash and scrounging to support his family. Gray finally landed a clerk's job but found his suit too big after years on relief diets. He conned a tailor to chalk on the alterations and had his wife do the sewing.

Gray spent eight months during this period upgrading his education at the Winnipeg Public Library. That's when he decided to become a journalist. He researched and wrote an article about racehorse doping and sold it to the *Winnipeg Free Press*. He would have framed the ten-dollar cheque, he said, but he needed the money to buy groceries.

That was in 1933. Two years later Gray started work at the *Free Press*, first as a reporter, at twenty dollars a week, then as an editorial writer in 1941, and Ottawa correspondent in 1947.

His focus was clear after he left Ottawa and moved to Calgary in 1948. He had spent a year, as he put it, "in a state of outraged indignation" over how little eastern politicians and journalists knew or cared about western Canada. He became editor of the *Farm and Ranch Review* and began supplying the eastern dailies with a regular column on western affairs.

During the years that followed, Gray continued to interpret the West for eastern readers. He worked in journalism until 1958, when he left his job as editor and publisher of the *Western Oil Examiner* to work for Home Oil as public relations manager.

Gray made good money at Home Oil, but he missed writing. He resubmitted his outline for *The Winter Years* to Macmillan, which had rejected the manuscript twenty years earlier. With publication finally a certainty, he took early retirement from Home Oil just to, as he said, complete this one book.

When the book came out in 1966, Gray—at age sixty—was on his way to becoming a best-selling author. By the mid-1970s, with a series of graphic, unconventional social histories of the Prairies under his belt, James H. Gray—as he identified himself on the book jackets—had become well established as western Canada's leading popular historian.

Gray was often referred to as a spokesman for "the West," but he dismissed the designation as geographically imprecise and culturally vague. He said he preferred the area to be called New Canada. "And the part of the New Canada turf that I have staked out for myself is the Great Plains country east of the Rockies."

Gray had a tongue-in-cheek suggestion as to how the CBC national news might more accurately reflect the concerns of New Canada in its coverage: "First, don't let anybody on the national news staff ever read the *Globe and Mail.* Second, don't let them ever watch U.S. television. Third, make them all read the front page of at least five major western papers daily."

Over a twenty-six-year period, Gray produced a dozen books, many of which became classics. They investigated aspects of prairie life that had until then received scant documentation. *Men Against the Desert* (1967) recorded how farm families fought drought, dust, insect infestations, and crop failures during the 1930s. *Red Lights on the Prairies* (1971) covered the story of prostitution before the depression. *Booze* (1972) took a critical look at the tradition of heavy drinking on the Prairies, refuting the long-held liberal view that Prohibition was a disaster.

His trademark was a vivid, eminently readable style, with solid research to counterbalance the personal reminiscences, and a sprinkling of sarcasm and mischievous wit.

In *Men Against the Desert*, he declared, "More lies have probably been told about the weather of the Dirty Thirties than any other subject except sex; yet most of the lies could have been true."

In *Red Lights on the Prairies*, he observed wickedly that, if other historians were to be believed, "monks, eunuchs, and vestal virgins" had settled the West.

Gray was unusual among historians in that he wrote chronicles of the common people rather than catalogues of politicians and acts of Parliament. "I don't give a damn about politicians," he said bluntly. "Ordinary people go through life without any awareness of politics at all."

But he did care about one politician: R.B. Bennett. He felt Bennett had been given a bum rap when he was characterized as the heartless villain of the depression, the penny-pinching Methodist who told Canadians they could resolve their economic problems by taking in one another's washing.

Gray didn't believe that Bennett's tightwad image was accurate. He had accidentally discovered, while researching a book about Alberta lawyers, that Bennett in private was the soul of generosity, a philanthropist who gave away thousands of dollars to worthy causes. How could such a man have earned a reputation as a destroyer of Canada? Gray vowed to rehabilitate the image, and he put forward the case that Bennett was "the most generous politician that ever lived in Canada." Like other Gray books, his *R.B. Bennett: The Calgary Years* was hailed by reviewers as a landmark contribution to the catalogue of Canadian history.

But Gray, who died in November 1998 at age ninety-two, will be remembered best for his other books, the books written for people who like history and don't like footnotes. His books are still in print, and they are still read. They always will be. It's not difficult to understand why Canada's National History Society awarded Jimmy Gray the Pierre Berton Award for popularizing Canadian history. When it came to telling the story to ordinary Canadians, nobody did it better.

Kerry Wood
Wildlife author and conservationist
1907–1998

Kerry Wood worked to protect the wilderness of central Alberta at a time when others sought to exploit it, and he made a living as a freelance writer at a time, during the Great Depression, when others said he should get a real job. Nobody would ever accuse this man of marching to the beat of someone else's drum.

Wood spent eighty-one of his ninety-one years in the Red Deer area. Born in New York City, he moved to Red Deer with his Scottish-born parents when he was ten. Seven years later, his parents asked him to move with them to the West Coast, where the climate would be better for his asthmatic mother. Kerry refused to go. He had decided to become an outdoors writer, and the parklands of the Red Deer region provided all the necessary raw materials: history, nature, and Native lore.

He had little training for the task beyond what he had learned in high school. "Educated myself—with help from hickory stick," he replied mischievously when the *Calgary Herald* asked him to provide details of his schooling. He did acknowledge, however, that "my scholarly father encouraged and guided me through a wide course of reading." Being part of a well-read family of church ministers and deacons also influenced him.

Inspired by the naturalist-philosopher Henry David Thoreau, Wood lived in the bush for twenty months after leaving high school and immersed himself in nature. He endured disease, loneliness, and starvation, and filled his notebooks with enough material to generate a series of stories for *Boy's Life*, a New York-based monthly magazine.

He quickly found his writing niche. By the time he was nineteen, Wood was selling stories to the *Saturday Evening Post* and writing regularly for the *Red Deer Advocate, Edmonton Bulletin, Edmonton Journal, Calgary Herald,* and *Calgary Albertan.* A California university offered him an honorary doctoral degree but he turned it down.

"He felt he didn't deserve it at such a young age," said his wife, the former Marjorie Marshall of Red Deer, whom he married in 1936.

Wood was one of the few Canadians to make a living from free-lance writing during the depression. He augmented his income by making archery tackle for mail-order sale, and toward the end of the 1930s he added further to his income by producing nature programs for CBC Radio. He later produced nature documentaries for CBC Television.

In 1945 Wood published his first book, *Three Mile Bend*, and earned a total of fifteen dollars in royalties. Two dozen more books followed. *Mickey the Beaver* (1946) became a Grade four reader in Canadian schools. *The Map-Maker* (1955), a book about explorer David Thompson, won the Governor-General's award for juvenile literature. A Governor-General's award also went to *The Great Chief* (1957), a book about Cree chief Maskepetoon.

Some of Wood's work found acceptance more readily in the United States than in Canada. In 1954 he published an autobiographical novel, *Wild Winter*, that told of a teenaged boy's struggle to survive in the bush during an Alberta winter. It took Wood eight years to get the book published in Canada after it appeared first in the United States. That was pretty typical, said Marjorie. "One has to be acclaimed outside the country before recognition comes at home."

As well as being a writer and broadcaster, Wood was a committed conservationist. His dedication to preserving natural habitat inspired the creation of dozens of wildlife sanctuaries throughout North America. He was front and centre in the movement to have the Gaetz Lakes area protected as a bird sanctuary and wildlife refuge. Others wanted to develop the untamed wilderness into a picnic ground or amusement park, but Wood saw the value of land in its natural state and fought to preserve it. "He was one of the first true environmentalists, before the movement became trendy," said Red Deer's municipal archivist, Michael Dawe.

Wood received wide recognition and numerous awards for his work, including an Alberta Achievement Award and the Order of Canada. The two that pleased him the most were the Canadian Authors' Association's Vicky Metcalf Award for "consistently good writing of material inspirational to Canadian youth" and an informal 1969 survey by Canadian librarians showing "that 500,000 children annually read my books."

In 1992 Wood donated his awards collection to the Red Deer museum and archives. After crunching the numbers, the archivists determined that he had written 6,200 short stories, 8,000 magazine articles, 9,000 newspaper columns, 4,000 radio scripts and 600 television scripts. He had gone through twenty typewriters, seen his stories appear in eighteen Canadian schoolbooks, and had them translated into several languages, including Braille.

His books, many coauthored with his wife, were mostly self-published. The task of marketing and selling them eventually became too arduous, so in the mid-1980s the couple donated more than two thousand volumes to elementary school libraries from Edmonton to Pincher Creek. This resulted in several requests for Kerry and Marjorie to give talks in the schools.

Wood continued to write into his late eighties. In 1995 Marjorie reported that "Nobby" (his family nickname) had one manuscript with an Edmonton publisher and was typing the final draft of another. He published his last book, *This Smiling Land*, in 1996 at age eighty-nine.

Wood died in July 1998 after battling heart disease and prostate cancer. The Order of Canada citation succinctly summarizes his impact: "An inspiration to naturalists around the world." Red Deer's Kerry Wood Drive and the Kerry Wood Nature Centre keep his name alive in his adopted community. The words of former Governor-General Ray Hnatyshyn put his achievement into perspective:

"At a time when the vast majority of people assumed that the environment could forever absorb the products and by-products of human existence, you were among the few who perceived the fragile nature of nature itself."

Alice Murdoch Adams

Dance teacher

1908–1997

Alice Murdoch Adams started Calgary's first school of ballet, tap, and Highland dance in the 1920s, creating a needed outlet for society's oldest form of artistic self-expression and establishing a tradition that continues to this day.

She was just fourteen when she dropped out of school and told her family she was going to become a dance teacher. That was not an easy thing to do in Calgary in 1922, especially given the limited opportunities for training and the fact that her family had no money for lessons. But Alice's passion for the oldest form of artistic self-expression could not be contained. She had taken Highland dance classes in her native Scotland before the family moved to Calgary, and she wanted to pick up where she had left off. She washed dishes at a downtown Calgary restaurant to pay for the lessons, and began her training with a dance instructor named Jean Gauld.

By age eighteen, Alice was on her way to success in her chosen field. She travelled for a year to the dance capitals of Europe and the United States to study dance in all its forms. In 1927 she returned to Calgary and opened the Alice Murdoch School of Dancing in the basement of her parents' home. Hers was the first school in the city to train students in different styles of dance and movement. Alice offered exercise and acrobatics classes as well as ballet, tap, Highland dance, and ballroom, and she taught all the classes herself.

She taught classes to children and adults. One of her adult students was an amateur boxer and gymnast named Bill Adams. He wasn't really interested in dance—he had enrolled in classes only to improve his footwork and agility. But he was a skilled gymnast and he could make Alice laugh. Their friendship grew into love and then marriage.

Bill worked as an electrician and radio repairmen while Alice continued to teach. She relocated her studio from her parents' home to a room over the Woolworth's store downtown. After that, she taught in her own home, using the living-room for lessons. She taught from September to June and spent the month of July taking lessons in New York. She used to joke that she timed the births of her first two children to happen in August so as not to interfere with either her teaching schedule or her annual pilgrimage to New York.

After teaching in Calgary for a few years, Alice opened a Lethbridge branch of her school, which was run by her assistant, Lola Strand. Alice took the train to Lethbridge to teach some of the classes, and she also taught in Drumheller, Claresholm, Stavely, Vulcan, and other rural communities. Asked what would happen if she ever got sick, Alice replied that she never got sick. "Or if I do, I just keep on teaching."

During the 1930s and 1940s, students of the Alice Murdoch School of Dancing were highly visible in Calgary. Their annual revues at the commodious Grand Theatre featured as many as 150 dancers accompanied by seven musicians. They performed forty-one different dances in each revue and played to audiences of one thousand or more. Alice also produced dance shows for the Palace and Capitol movie theatres. The thirty-minute shows were presented as a warm-up attraction before the films, and the dances had to be linked in some manner to the theme of the feature movie. This wasn't always easy to do, but Alice always managed. She also designed and cut the patterns for her dancers' costumes, while her parents and friends did the sewing.

During the war years, Alice produced a dance show that played at army, air force, and prisoner of war camps throughout Alberta. Between 1939 and 1943, her troupes performed about four hundred shows. The government paid for transportation and food, and the dancers volunteered their time as part of the war effort. They travelled by bus, returning to Calgary after each show. Alice's son Ron toured with the troupe as soon as he was old enough to play the accordion. During this time Alice also produced the downtown Rotary Club's annual president's ball, an event that she continued to choreograph for several years after the war.

After undergoing back surgery in 1949, Alice put away her ballet slippers and tap shoes and thought her dancing days were behind her.

She turned the operation of the school over to her younger sister Jean, a world champion Highland dancer and tap specialist. She had worked seven days a week for more than twenty years and raised two children. Her husband told her she had earned her rest.

Alice's daughter Vicki was born the year she retired from the dance school, and Alice thought at first that she would not put Vicki into dance. But Vicki was born to dance. When she saw her Aunt Jean teaching classes, she begged for lessons, and Alice became involved again. She saw her daughter's passion for dance and took on a new role—as a dance mom.

Like her mother, Vicki Adams Willis became a dance teacher and choreographer. She also travelled to New York and Europe, as her mother had done, and returned to Calgary to teach at the University of Calgary for fifteen years. She left the university in 1984 to co-found, with two of her graduate students, a company named Decidedly Jazz Danceworks. It has carved a niche for itself in the heart of Canada's dance world as the only professional company devoted to jazz dance.

Alice Adams never really retired from dance after that first short-lived attempt in 1949. At age eighty-two, when she was given the Alberta Dance Alliance's first Alberta Dance Award, she told friends she was still "choreographing a little dance, just for fun." She was embarrassed to receive the award as she hadn't been prominent on the dance scene for forty years. How would anyone possibly care? But the dance community does not forget its own. Alice agreed to accept the award as long as she didn't have to make a speech, and the Alberta dance community was able to celebrate the life and work of one of its earliest pioneers.

Alice died in November 1997 at age eighty-nine. Her daughter continues to run Decidedly Jazz Danceworks, together with co-founders Michele Moss and Hannah Stilwell, carrying on a family tradition that began with her mother's Calgary dance studio in the 1920s. The dance styles have changed and so has the music, but, as choreographer Anne Flynn has written, "Something in the spirit of Alice Murdoch's work is being kept alive every time her daughter begins that familiar count to eight."

Arnold Platt

Agricultural scientist

1909–1996

It took Arnold Platt more than five years of arduous, painstaking, and often discouraging crop breeding work—starting in 1938—to develop the first variety of Canadian wheat resistant to a destructive wasp-like insect known as the sawfly.

But his persistence paid off. In 1944 Platt was hailed around the world as the saviour of the prairie wheatlands. Saskatchewan named two of its lakes—Platt and Rescue—in appreciation of his work, and the University of Alberta granted him an honorary doctorate.

Platt named the wheat he genetically engineered "rescue" because it promised to rescue 13 million acres of wheatlands in Saskatchewan and southern Alberta from potential sawfly ruin. It would also rescue the prairie farm economy from millions of dollars in losses.

Platt was an impatient achiever. He grew irritable if he wasn't involved in trying to solve a problem of some kind, usually to do with farming. He was born on a farm near Innisfree, 120 kilometres east of Edmonton, and he always thought of farming as a noble calling. It was more than just raising wheat, cattle, and hogs, he said. "It is also raising scientists, statesmen, and humanitarians."

Platt was a scientist—of the agricultural kind. He graduated from the University of Alberta at age twenty-six with degrees in genetics and plant breeding, and went to work as an agriculture researcher at the federal government's experimental farm in Swift Current, Saskatchewan. His first assignment was to find a solution to the sawfly problem that was costing western wheat farmers $20 million annually. The problem had confounded the best scientific minds around. Platt promised to do what he could to save the land.

Farmers were losing their crops to a yellow-and-black insect that laid its eggs inside the hollow stem of the wheat plant. The larvae migrated to the base of the plant and sawed through it until it collapsed on the ground, where no harvesting machine could pick it up.

Platt thought he might solve the problem by developing a strain of wheat with a solid stem. The sawfly would have to lay its eggs elsewhere, and the wheat would no longer be vulnerable. Working with a small research team, he spent the Second World War years looking for a solution. He experimented with wheat varieties from around the world and finally found two that would cross to produce the desired result. At first only about one in seven hundred genetically engineered plants showed the required resistance to the sawfly, but gradually the numbers improved and the team reported the success. Their victory was heralded around the world.

A few years later, Platt decided it was time for him to start farming. He moved to the Lethbridge area and became active in the Farmers' Union of Alberta as a passionate advocate for farmers. They were, he said, a "proud, freedom-loving people whose daily work is done in an atmosphere of thought and meditation." Governments might think of farmers as a special interest group always looking for subsidies but, to Platt, they were a "great forum of people uniquely endowed to give more than their share to humanity."

Platt became president of the Farmers' Union and an adviser to the Canadian Wheat Board in 1956. He served as a member of the Canadian delegation that negotiated an international wheat agreement in Geneva in 1959, and also served as a member of a royal commission that studied the impact of freight rates on prairie agriculture. Several years later he chaired a committee that led to the formation of Unifarm, the giant umbrella group of Alberta farm organizations. He also played a central role in the formation of the Alberta Cattle Commission.

During a land acquisition dispute between Hutterites and farmers in the 1970s, Platt acted as mediator for the Alberta government. The Hutterites were buying large tracts of provincial land to accommodate colony expansion, and farmers felt threatened by their expansion. Platt resolved the dispute by convincing the farmers that, while the Hutterites did own large amounts of land, they also contributed more than their proportional share of agricultural produce within the provincial farming economy.

Also during the 1970s, Platt chaired the public hearings into the proposed construction of the Oldman River dam, a development upstream of Pincher Creek designed to supply irrigation and municipal water supplies to Lethbridge and adjacent areas of southern Alberta. The dam aroused considerable controversy, with opponents claiming serious adverse effects on river habitat, archaeological sites, and trout fishing. Proponents saw the expansion of irrigation development and increased certainty of water supplies as benefits that outweighed environmental concerns.

In 1973 Platt moved to Cardston, where he lived for twenty years, and ran an agricultural consulting agency. He retired from his active agricultural involvements during the 1980s but maintained his interest in farming until the day he died. When his eyesight began to fail, his wife, Helen, read to him from the farm journals.

At age eighty-five, Platt decided to make a return trip to southwestern Saskatchewan to see how the land was doing all these years after the eradication of the sawfly problem. He found the area thriving with prosperous farms. As he looked out over a flourishing tract of prairie wheatland, and got down on his hands and knees to feel and smell the earth, he realized his dream had not been impossible. His long-ago promise to save the land—a promise given more in hope than in certainty—had truly been fulfilled. Platt died the following spring.

Nicholas Morant

Photographer

1910–1999

A passenger train steams through the Rockies, headlights glistening as it sweeps around the bend. This defining image of the Canadian Pacific Railway was captured during the 1930s by a self-taught photographer named Nicholas Morant. He learned his craft by trial and error and spent fifty-one years working for the railway company as a designated "special cameraman."

Morant was indeed special, as his legacy would indicate. He created some of the most spectacular photographs ever taken of trains and their surroundings. At the height of his career, during the 1940s and 1950s, his images graced not only CPR brochures but also *National Geographic* covers, postage stamps, chinaware, chocolate boxes, and the backs of Canadian banknotes. "You can hardly go into a store anywhere and not see one of my pictures," he said in 1959, and nobody disputed his claim.

Though he took pictures of subjects other than trains, Morant will be remembered for his railway photography. "He had the railway in his blood," said Robert J. Ritchie, president and chief executive officer of CP Rail. "But he helped define more than the railway. He was mainly responsible for creating the visual history that western Canada has now."

It's unclear how Morant ever managed to convince the railway company, during the height of the depression, to hire him as a full-time photographer. But convince them he did, and so he traded his CPR publicity writer's job in Winnipeg for a job in Banff taking pictures of trains. He settled in the mountain community with his wife, the former Ivy Young, whom he enigmatically referred to as "Willie," and walked almost every mile of the CP line between Calgary and Vancouver in his quest for the perfect photograph.

He found his ideal location at a lookout on Highway 1A, five kilometres east of Lake Louise. "What better location have you got?"

he said. "The river is always open in the winter here because it's fast flowing. You've got the scenery, the S-shaped track—everything." He used the lookout so many times for his CP Rail promotional photos that it eventually became known as Morant's Curve.

His assignment involved taking pictures of trains, but Morant knew it was much more than that. It was also about romance, adventure, and beauty. The mountains, rivers, lakes, forests, and prairies of Canada were as important an element in his pictures as the rolling stock in the foreground.

If his job seemed idyllic—taking picture-postcard shots of trains, trees, and mountains—it was not as easy as some might have thought. Morant lugged heavy camera equipment up mountain passes and across the tops of tunnels, and often waited for hours on bitter winter days to capture the image he wanted. When a train approached, he usually had just one chance to make the shot. "It was miserable, of course," he said. "You didn't know when the freights were coming for sure, so you couldn't stay warm in the car."

Morant's one-shot images documented Canadian history as it was being made. Pictures of freight cars loaded with Canmore coal in the 1950s served as a reminder that the mountain community did not start out as a tourist destination. Pictures of steam locomotives taken in Montreal during the 1960s showed the once state-of-the-art engines as the silent victims of the diesel revolution. "He had a complete command of the decisive moment of Canadian photography," said Banff historian Robert Sandford. "He never wasted film, and didn't blanket-shoot events like many contemporary photographers do. Instead, he waited for the precise moment when the best image could be made."

Sometimes his work could be dangerous. In 1939 Morant survived a grizzly bear attack while on assignment in Yoho National Park. "Anyone who puts his life on the line for a picture is crazy as hell," he said afterwards. He spent nine months in hospital recovering from scalp lacerations, ripped leg muscles, and a broken arm. Because of his injuries, he was unable to serve in the armed forces during the Second World War. Instead, he worked for the government wartime information service, taking pictures of military vessels.

Notwithstanding his comment about not putting his life on the line, Morant did risk danger on more than one occasion. He came close to falling off the tower of the Royal Bank building in Edmonton while shooting pictures at night, and he almost died in a mountain chasm while lowering himself down by rope to get a better angle for a photo. "That one just about scared me to death," he said. To make matters worse, "they never used the shot."

But that photo was one of his few rejections. Dozens of magazines, including *Time, Life,* and *Fortune,* showcased Morant's work. One of his photos of Lake Louise was the only Canadian print chosen for a *National Geographic* exhibition of the best one hundred photos of the twentieth century. His black-and-white photo of a steam locomotive emerging from a mountain tunnel became well known as the cover shot of Pierre Berton's best-selling book *The National Dream* and also as the promotional art for the popular television series of the same name.

Most of Morant's thousands of photos of the Canadian Rockies were preserved after he retired from CP Rail in 1980. About fourteen thousand negatives are housed in the CP Rail archives, and another twenty thousand are on file at the National Film Board in Ottawa. Morant's images can also be found in such books as *Nicholas Morant's Canadian Pacific* and *Nicholas Morant's Canada.*

Morant received the Order of Canada in 1990. When a Calgary newspaper phoned him for a reaction, he used a line that he said he had been carrying around in his head for years: "Never forget that the greatest thing about photography is the glorious uncertainty of it."

He died in March 1999 at age eighty-eight. "I always said I let the mountains do all the work," Morant had said when he retired. "The railway opened up all this incredible country, and it was my job to take photos to sell it to the public. Not a bad way to earn a living, is it?"

Melvin "Fritz" Hanson

Football player

1912–1996

When Fritz Hanson played in the Canadian Football League for Winnipeg and Calgary during the 1930s and 1940s, he created such excitement that the sportswriters were unable to settle on just one nickname for him. They had to give him several: Twinkletoes, Fritzie, the Golden Ghost, and the Perlham Palehead. Taken all together, the nicknames meant that Hanson was a golden-haired athlete from Perlham, Minnesota, who ran like the wind and danced around the field with the grace and agility of a professional dancer.

Hanson was what the sportswriters characterized as an "import," one of a number of American marquee players brought up to add lustre to Canadian football. After making his name as a running back at North Dakota State University, where he once scored eleven touchdowns in a single game, he was wooed by the Detroit Lions, who offered him $125 a game to play in the National Football League. But Hanson opted for the Winnipeg Football Club, which offered him a depression-era windfall of $150 a game. Plus, he could work at the Winnipeg Grain Exchange for an additional $100 a month.

Hanson helped turn the annual Grey Cup game into a national event in 1935. He starred on the Winnipeg team that defeated the Hamilton Tigers 18–12, and brought the trophy west for the first time. Headline writers called it the "Fritz Blitz." On a slippery, icy field, Hanson racked up 305 yards on kick returns, including a seventy-eight-yard touchdown trip that wrapped up the game for his team. The fans went wild and Grey Cup fever was born.

Hanson's memorable performance in that game brought him lasting glory in Winnipeg, where he continued to shine. He made the all-star team every season through 1941, when he became a Canadian citizen and enlisted in the army. He returned to the Winnipeg back-field after the war, and a local newspaper columnist reported that "Twinkletoes Hanson showed he could still twinkle by setting up the

Bombers's first major with a fifty-two-yard run without the benefit of blocking."

At the end of the 1945 season, Hanson announced he was going to quit the game for good. He moved to Calgary and joined the insurance brokerage firm Reed, Shaw, McNaught. But he wasn't quite through with football. He signed with the Calgary Stampeders to prove that his legs could still handle the broken-field running plays that had dazzled fans and confounded opponents during his career in Winnipeg. In 1948, at age thirty-six, Hanson played on the Stampeders team that defeated Ottawa 12–7 and brought the Grey Cup to Calgary for the first time.

Hanson hung up his battered leather helmet in 1949 and set down roots in Calgary with his wife, Maxine. Every summer he helped out with the Stampede parade, and every fall he hunted waterfowl near Hanna with a group of close friends. During the 1950s, the hunting party included Bing Crosby, with whom Hanson shared a love of crooning. Friends recalled that when the bosses from Winnipeg had first gone to North Dakota to discuss terms with Hanson, they had found the young football player sitting atop a piano in a Fargo bar, leading the customers in song. Hanson was among the first volunteers to raise money in Calgary for Ducks Unlimited, a conservation group that has spent millions on waterfowl habitat projects.

Hanson was a vice president with Reed, Shaw, McNaught when he turned sixty-five. Although he retired from the firm twice, he never stopped coming into the office. He told friends that he was happy to be able to swim for free in the municipal pools and ride for free on public transit because he was now a senior citizen.

When Hanson died of cancer in 1996 at age eighty-three, his impact on Canadian football had largely been forgotten. National coverage of his death was limited to a small story in the *Globe and Mail* eight days after the obituary notices were published in Calgary newspapers. But some sportswriters remembered when Twinkletoes was bigger than Gretzky. "He lived his full eighty-three years exuberantly," wrote veteran Vancouver columnist Jim Coleman. "His was a blithe spirit."

Fred C. Mannix

Businessman

1913–1995

The gravestone of Fred Charles Mannix bears his name, the years he lived, and a simple one-word epitaph: "Builder." That simply describes the role he played in life, but it tells us nothing about the man himself. He would have wanted it that way.

In the history of Calgary's very rich and very private Mannix family, it is often difficult to separate legend from fact. One story has it that when Fred Charles was a young teenager he went to work on his father's construction sites, drank whisky and played poker, had his nose broken five times in fist fights, and smashed up several of the automobiles his father gave him as gifts. True or not, the story adds to the mystique of the hard-nosed businessman who wrestled back the construction company his father had sold to an American company, and built it into a multinational conglomerate that at one time controlled as many as 132 firms.

Fred Charles was the only son of Fred Stephen Mannix, a Manitoba farm boy of Irish parentage who followed the Canadian Pacific Railway construction into Alberta in the early 1900s, settled in Calgary in 1914, and went broke three times before making his fortune in construction and coal.

Fred Charles, born into what could have been a life of privilege, was educated privately at boarding schools in Calgary, Regina, and Mill Bay, British Columbia. He might have gone into his father's business without ever getting his hands dirty, but Fred Stephen didn't believe in making things so easy for his son. He had been making his way in the world since he left home at fourteen, and he expected his son to learn a thing or two at the same school of hard knocks.

The senior Mannix had his son working summers on his construction sites by the time he was thirteen and, at the end of the day, he put the family-owned company just beyond his son's reach by selling it to Idaho construction giant Morrison-Knudsen. Fred Charles, however, was an astute businessman. By 1953, thanks to smart investing in Alberta's expanding oil business, he was able to buy back the Mannix family firm.

From the 1950s onward, Fred Charles, with little or no public fanfare, built an impressive chunk of Canada's infrastructure through his various companies. Officially, the companies were known collectively as Loram—short for "Long Range Mannix"—but Fred Charles and his employees always referred to them simply as "the outfit."

The outfit worked on projects as diverse as the Toronto subway system, the St. Lawrence Seaway, the Trans-Canada Highway, the Comox airport, the Great Canadian Oil Sands plant, and the Baie Comeau Wharf. It also built the Pembina pipeline to carry Alberta oil to markets in central Canada. Through Manalta Coal, the outfit supplied fuel for three-quarters of the electrical generating plants in Alberta.

Fred Charles operated under a veil of secrecy that shrouded both his business and his private life. Because Loram was not publicly traded, Mannix felt he had to answer to no one, least of all to the press. The corporate empire employed four full-time public relations officers whose job was to keep the Mannix name out of print. When author Diane Francis asked to interview a company executive while researching her book *Controlling Interests: Who Owns Canada?*, the response was characteristic: "An interview? No way!" replied PR chief Linda Buckley. "I've never issued a press release in eight years." Another PR head, David Wood, spent thirteen years with the outfit without ever having any direct dealings with the press. "Although by title I was the director of public relations," he said, "in actuality, I was the editor of the company magazine."

The secrecy inevitably gave rise to speculation. Observers spoke of the ruthlessness Fred Charles must have used to become a construction magnate, the unwavering fidelity he demanded from his employees, and the influence he exerted in the back rooms of Alberta politics, especially after his former company secretary Peter Lougheed became premier in 1971.

Many of the people who worked with Mannix went on to become key members of the Alberta establishment. Aside from Lougheed, the most notable included Harold Milavsky, president of Trizec, Stan

Waters, Canada's only elected senator, and Robert Kramer, the founder of Kramer Tractor.

Lougheed said that Fred Charles "was like a brother to me, and we travelled the world together." During some of those trips, according to Lougheed, Mannix went "eyeball to eyeball with the big eastern corporations—and they blinked." But Fred Charles didn't always get his way. The day after Lougheed won the 1971 election, Mannix visited the new premier in his office and wrote some names on a piece of paper. "This," he declared, tossing the paper onto Lougheed's desk, "is your cabinet." Lougheed was noncommittal. Not one name from the Mannix list made that first Alberta Conservative cabinet.

Lougheed biographer Alan Hustak, one of the few reporters ever granted an audience with Mannix, believes that his obsession with secrecy was rooted in his fear of being kidnapped. The fear was validated in 1972, when the seventeen-year-old daughter of Sam Hashman, a developer friend, was held for ransom. When the girl was rescued and the kidnappers arrested, police discovered that the real target had been Mannix's wife, Margaret. After that, Mannix took extraordinary precautions to ensure only the right people could get close to him.

Hustak interviewed Mannix in 1976 while researching his Lougheed biography, and found him to be a "very brusque character" who referred to journalists as "pencil pushers" and docked pay from his public relations staff whenever an unauthorized story about him appeared in the press. "I would never want to be on the wrong end of Fred C. Mannix," said Hustak. "He reminded me of a sixteenth-century pirate, a privateer turned prelate."

By the same token, said Hustak, Mannix was an extraordinarily benevolent philanthropist who gave to charities, to universities, and directly to people in need. The only condition was that if they revealed the source of the gift, they forfeited it. "His works of generosity and kindness, done quietly without anybody knowing, are countless and legendary," said Hustak.

Calgarians caught a rare public glimpse of the reclusive tycoon in 1981 after he sued the Lougheed government for more compensation for the 327 acres of Mannix ranch property that had been expropriated to build Fish Creek Provincial Park on Calgary's southern edge.

The government offered $5 million for the land. Mannix sued for an additional $35.8 million.

When he testified at the trial, the businessman did not look anything like the "sixteenth-century pirate" Hustak had described. The formerly piercing, steel-blue eyes had grown dim and tearful. Gaunt and frail, weakened by the effects of two heart attacks and numerous strokes, Mannix told the court of his strong sentimental attachment to the land. After numerous appeals, he was awarded $7 million in 1984.

Failing health forced Mannix to withdraw from active involvement in the outfit. He turned the day-to-day operations over to his sons Fred Philip and Ron Neil and began to focus more on his family foundation's charitable giving. One of the foundation's gifts to Calgary was the $700,000 Carthy organ installed in the Jack Singer Concert Hall in 1987. When a reporter asked about the Carthy name, the Mannix people seemed embarrassed and gave no reply. It was later discovered that the name should have been McCarthy— after Fred Charles's Irish ancestor, Elizabeth Mannix McCarthy. A Mannix foundation employee had spelled the name wrong.

Fred Charles spent his last years dividing his time between his golf cottage in Palm Desert and the family's ranch property south of Calgary, where, according to a friend, he had three separate wine cellars in the basement to maintain various vintages at different temperatures.

He died in July 1995 at age eighty-one. His wife Margaret, whom he had married in 1939, predeceased him in 1979. His second marriage, to the former Janice Florendine, ended in divorce.

The *Calgary Herald* obituary described Fred Charles as an "industrial pioneer and humanitarian who preferred anonymity." He was buried in a small cemetery near Millarville, southwest of Calgary.

Violet Archer

Composer

1913–2000

American composer Aaron Copland once said, "Women do not make good composers." Violet Archer proved him wrong. She did so as one of the few Canadian classical composers to make an impact outside Canada, and she did so while living in Alberta, a place where one does not normally expect to find native-born composers of international significance.

Archer lived in Edmonton for most of her working life as a musician, teacher, and composer. Born Violetta Balestreri in Montreal in 1913, she became Violet Archer in 1940 when her Italian family chose a surname to correspond with the English translation of Balestreri—"crossbow." She started learning piano when she was nine, played percussion in an all-female orchestra as a teenager, and was sixteen when "the composing bug hit me." Tennyson's poem *The Splendour Falls on Castle Walls* inspired her to compose her first tone poem. She subsequently wrote music based on poems by e.e. cummings and Irving Layton.

Archer began composing just for the sake of composing. She never expected to hear her orchestral or small-group ensemble music played for an audience. "So I never worried about performance to the extent that it would do anything to the way I felt about composing. As soon as I finished one piece, there was another one to write." She composed all the music in her head ("not like the Hollywood image of a composer sitting at the piano, playing notes, and writing them down") and asked her mother to wake her at dawn every day so she could sit on the balcony creating music.

After composing her first piece, Archer knew exactly what she wanted to do with her life. She paid for her classes at the McGill University music school by working as an accompanist, and derived so much satisfaction from her composition studies with the Montreal-born composer Claude Champagne that she continued studying through the summer. "I couldn't bear to be away from composing," she said.

Archer graduated from McGill in 1936 with a degree in composition and a teacher's certificate in piano. Two years later, she earned a teaching diploma from the Royal Canadian College of Organists, and a few years after that, she began commuting to New York to study with the Hungarian-born composer Bela Bartok. He did not take many female students, but after examining Archer's compositions, he accepted her.

Bartok taught her the importance of putting a personal stamp on her composing and of not becoming a slave to musical fashion. Archer always remembered this advice. Over the years she created a body of work that she considered distinctively Canadian, with such titles as *Prairie Profiles, Northern Landscape,* and *Proud Horses.* "I felt in harmony with the great landscapes we have in this country," she said. Critics praised her for expressing the "vastness and newness" of Canada.

Archer earned her master's degree at Yale in the late 1940s. Because she hadn't been able to afford the bus fare to Massachusetts to write the entrance exam, she had persuaded the university authorities to let her write the exam in Montreal. She did so well on the exam that she won a scholarship to Yale and had an opportunity to study composition with the German-born modern composer Paul Hindemith. He encouraged her to think about economy in her composing and to make every note count. "Do lots with little," he told her.

In 1950 Archer became teacher and composer in residence at North Texas State College. She also taught at the University of Oklahoma and at Cornell University. Then, in 1962, came an opportunity to start a graduate program in musical theory and composition at the University of Alberta in Edmonton. It was a very good move for her, she said. "There was a real opportunity there for growth. It wasn't a very big department when I arrived."

She spent sixteen years at the University of Alberta, and many of her students—including Allan Bell, Vernon Murgatroyd, Allan Gilliland, and Robert Rosen—went on to make their own important contributions to the Canadian classical music scene. "Former students were devoted to her, and the devotion went both ways," said Allan Bell.

Archer retired from the university in 1978, but she remained in Edmonton for the next twenty years, writing her compositions and spending time as composer in residence at the Banff Centre.

She taught privately and remained an active composer until the day she died. "It's what I was born to do," she said. Archer composed an estimated four hundred works, including pieces for orchestra, voice, choir, organ, piano, and chamber groups. She wrote two operas and more than ninety children's songs, composed the soundtracks for two Canadian documentaries, and had her music performed in more than three dozen countries. "She was one of the first to link Canada to the rest of the classical music world," said Edmonton music critic D. T. Baker.

Orchestras and chamber ensembles across the country and abroad regularly performed Archer's music. In 1993, just before she turned eighty, her piece entitled *Variations on an Original Theme for Carillon* was played on the carillon at the Peace Tower in Ottawa. "I've been fortunate that my music has drawn enough attention to be played on a fairly large scale," she said. Among those who often performed her work were Canadian cellist Shauna Rolston and Calgary jazz saxophone quartet the Swinging Bovines.

Archer wrote for every orchestral instrument—including one piece for solo snare drum—except the double bassoon. Her last commissioned work, completed in 1999, was a concerto for accordion and orchestra. "I don't hate the accordion, but it is a challenge," she said.

In 1998 Archer left Edmonton and moved to Ottawa to be closer to her family. She became adjunct professor of music at Carleton University, adjudicated a competition for composers of children's music, and kept right on composing. "For me, it's as necessary as breathing."

Archer never married. She shared her household with two fat Siamese cats, Sonatina and Fuguetta. "She was completely absorbed by music—and cats," her friend Isobel Rolston told an Ottawa newspaper.

Archer died in Ottawa at age eighty-six. Her legacy includes the

Violet Archer Library at the Canadian Music Centre's Calgary office, which she endowed with $50,000, and two scholarships at the University of Alberta. "She created an impressive body of work," said John Reid of the Canadian Music Centre. "And what's more, it's still being performed."

Harry Strom

Farmer and premier of Alberta

1914–1984

Harry Strom had some mighty big shoes to fill when he became Social Credit premier of Alberta in 1968. His predecessor, Ernest C. Manning, had been one of Canada's most effective provincial leaders, winning seven consecutive elections, ruling for twenty-five years, and retiring at the peak of his power. Manning, in turn, had inherited the mantle of Social Credit from William Aberhart, the radio evangelist who first brought the party to power in 1935.

Strom came from the same evangelical background as Manning and Aberhart. Born on a farm near Burdett, halfway between Lethbridge and Medicine Hat, he was the son of Swedish-born immigrants who moved from Minnesota to southern Alberta during the early 1900s, and he was active in the Evangelical Free Church.

His mother moved the family to Calgary in 1928 after Strom's father died. During the depression he was shocked to see "businessmen wearing white shirts out digging ditches." He trained as an auto mechanic at the Southern Alberta Institute of Technology, worked as a truck driver, then returned to Burdett to become a farmer.

Strom said he never sought political office, but he became a municipal councillor when he was in his early twenties. "My neighbours asked me to run." He ran for divisional school board when they asked him to become a school trustee, and he served as chairman of the local rural electrification association. He was also involved in water conservation.

Strom became the Socred member of the legislative assembly for Cypress in 1955, when he was forty-one, and said he could hardly believe how his political career had evolved. "Never did I expect to be called on to assume greater responsibilities," he said. He was re-elected by a large majority in 1959.

In 1962 Premier Manning named Strom agriculture minister. Over the next five years, Strom revamped the agriculture department, created a system of provincial marketing boards for agricultural produce, and encouraged the expansion of agricultural research.

He became municipal affairs minister in 1968, the year Manning resigned with no designated successor. Strom was encouraged to run for the leadership, and he defeated party veteran Gordon Taylor and three other candidates. At fifty-four, Strom was ushered into the premier's chair by supporters who considered him best suited to follow Manning. But he was too much the team player and Manning loyalist to be anything more than a caretaker premier. "It's not a question of whether or not I can fill Mr. Manning's shoes," he said, "because I don't think there is anyone who can." Strom was content to operate in Manning's shadow until the voters found a new Moses to lead them.

During his three years as premier, Strom found it difficult to follow the course set by Manning against forces that threatened Social Credit principles. Cautious financial conservatism and social reformism had marked Manning's stewardship. He had succeeded with a steady record of pay-as-you-go government. Strom faced a growing demand for government services regardless of price. The rising costs of health, education, and welfare threatened the pay-as-you-go policy. While he still believed in controlling government growth and spending, Strom's humanitarian concern would not allow him to ignore those who truly needed help. "Security with freedom for the individual" was what he advocated.

Strom lost the 1971 election to Peter Lougheed, an ambitious forty-three-year-old lawyer and former football player who rallied his supporters with the war cry, "Time for a change. Now!" A restless and changing Alberta was seeking new faces and new solutions to the province's political problems, and Social Credit no longer had the answers.

The fact that Strom had established Alberta's environment department and brought in other social reforms was not enough. He had become the pan-piper of Alberta politics at a time when the voters wanted to hear trumpets. Lougheed had the right combination of brass and wind, and the electorate voted accordingly. They had found their new Moses.

Strom's defeat was less a personal loss for the man than a triumph for a new-ideas party that convinced the voters, in Lougheed's much-quoted line, that "everything is not just great in good old Alberta."

Strom's party, though out of power for the first time in thirty-six years, never rejected him. They allowed the soft-spoken politician to sit as Opposition leader for more than a year, until he decided it was time to return to the agricultural world he had come from.

Strom went back to his Burdett farm for a few years, then spent his final years, until his death from cancer at age seventy, quietly serving meals at an Edmonton church mission for the poor. He had never really set out to be premier, he told a reporter in a rare interview given after he left politics. "One thing just led to another."

After he died, in Edmonton in October 1984, he was remembered as a man of integrity and decency whose personal qualities might have brought him lasting political success in other circumstances. Among those paying tribute was New Democratic leader Grant Notley, who would die in a plane crash just two weeks later. The reluctant politician from Burdett, said Notley, had been a "gentleman of Christian values who never lost his humility despite holding high office."

At the time of Strom's death, there was little left of the once-mighty Social Credit party. The party ran no candidates in the 1986 provincial election and fielded only six in the 1989 election. In 1992 it revived itself under the leadership of Randy Thorsteinson, a Red Deer travel agent, and once again it started attracting candidates, cash, and attention. In 1997 the Socreds ran seventy candidates in Alberta's eighty-three ridings. They still did not win any seats, but they placed third in the popular vote after the Tories and the Liberals. At that point, the political pundits spoke of Thorsteinson—who subsequently resigned in a dispute over his Mormon beliefs—as being heir to the throne of Aberhart and Manning. They did not mention the man who had been the last Social Credit premier of Alberta. Such good as Strom did was interred with his bones.

Jimmy "the Con" Carleton
Reformed felon and anti-poverty activist
1914–1992

Jimmy the Con was a two-bit fraud artist who spent twenty-five years of his life behind bars, parlayed his experiences into a job as guest lecturer on crime, and gave newspapers a most unforgettable character to write about.

Reporters couldn't get enough of him. He had once been a reporter himself, he said, and that appealed to them. A crime reporter who became a criminal—how could they resist such a story? When he ran for mayor of Calgary, they knew he didn't have a chance, but they wrote about him anyhow. He was a character, and characters make for better copy than people in suits who talk about fiscal responsibility and strategic initiatives.

The press first discovered Jimmy in 1979, when he was living in the Calgary provincial correctional centre, serving the last of his 485 jail sentences for fraud. He always opted for jail, he said, because he could never afford to pay the fines. While out on a day pass, he spoke to a University of Calgary criminology class and that's how he first made the news.

Everything about him invited attention, starting with his appearance. His white hair stood out from his head as if he had just plunged his fingers into a light socket. His front teeth were a distant memory, and he always wore carpet slippers, even in the middle of winter. Why? Nobody ever found out. Reporters tried to top one another with their descriptions of him, but Jimmy himself had the best one of all: "Like Beethoven on a drunk."

Then came the biographical details, which invariably differed from story to story. In the most colourful of them, Jimmy was a robber baron's son from St. Louis whose mother had died giving birth to him in a private railway carriage. He ran away to Canada when he was fifteen and turned to a life of crime to pay for his first wife's drug habit. In another story, he was a drifter from small-town Ontario without any connections to ill-gotten American wealth. But that one made for duller copy.

The matrimonial details provided additional embroidery: Five ex-wives and forty-two children, said Jimmy. His sixth wife, Irene Kotliarevski, was fifty-one years his junior, and they had two daughters together. "He's a child trapped in a man's body," said Irene.

They met, she said, while he was giving a lecture at Simon Fraser University in British Columbia. She worked at the university as a volunteer Russian interpreter. He pledged his love in the university coffee shop three days after they met. "Why don't we wait?" suggested Irene. Jimmy replied, "I'm sixty-eight. I don't have that kind of time." Three months later, they married.

In the beginning, the couple travelled together as partners in crime. He taught her everything he knew. He had started writing bad cheques, he said, to cover the shortfall between his forty-three-dollar-a-week salary at the *Winnipeg Free Press* and the cost of his first wife's prescription pills. She worked the night shift at a local hospital and took the pills to stay awake. Over time she became addicted to stronger and stronger drugs. Jimmy estimated that he stole $2.5 million, all to pay for her habit. "I didn't keep any of it."

Just as Jimmy always went to jail for his crimes, so too did Irene. They pleaded guilty to writing $4,500 in bad cheques and did their time. When they came out, they ran a highway truck stop—daringly named Jimmy the Con's Roadside Diner—near Champion, southeast of High River. After losing the diner in a dispute with the power company over unpaid bills, they moved to Calgary.

Jimmy resumed his life of crime for a while, but now it was time for him to do something that would keep him out of jail. He hosted a cable talk show and became something of a local celebrity. He and Irene became community activists, fighting to keep an inner-city school from closing and a mall on the banks of the Bow River from opening. Then, much to the delight of the reporters who had tracked his every move since he had returned to Calgary, Jimmy announced he was running for an independent seat in Parliament. "Yes, I stole money," he acknowledged. "But I never stole from people, only from banks."

When he predictably lost the federal race, he turned his attention to the local political scene. Ralph Klein had left the mayor's office to move into provincial politics, and Jimmy decided to become his replacement. His major fund-raiser would be a seven-day hot tub party in his back yard, he said, and he would work for the poor and the needy. And just in case anyone should fail to recognize his name on the electoral ballot, he listed himself as Jimmy "the Con" Carleton.

He lost the mayor's race to Al Duerr but captured an impressive number of votes. A former school board chair, Anne Tingle, finished behind him. Jimmy quipped that if he had started in politics at age twenty-five, "I'd now be prime minister."

He suggested that Duerr pay him $52,000 to tackle the city's poverty problem, but the mayor wasn't interested. Undeterred, Jimmy set up his own foundation to help the poor and announced he would run against Duerr again in the 1992 mayoralty race.

Jimmy died before he had a chance to take out nomination papers. His death, as bizarre as his life, occurred after an inebriated fall down the icy back steps outside his Calgary home.

Cops, lawyers, politicians, courthouse workers, and Jimmy's barroom pals attended the funeral. The presiding preacher suggested that the Con's nickname be retired, and that he be known thenceforth as Jimmy the Helpful because he had worked for those less fortunate than himself. However, it's hard to rewrite the past, especially when that past might have come out of the pages of Damon Runyon. Jimmy the Con will live forever in the memories of veteran Calgary reporters as the man who was always guaranteed to bring colour to a grey news day.

Irene McCaugherty

Folk artist and writer

1914–1996

A field of history awaited harvesting in Irene McCaugherty's corner of southern Alberta, and she used every tool at her disposal—writing, photography, and painting—to do the cutting and the reaping.

The writing came first. Born and raised on a homestead near Lethbridge, Irene suffered from loneliness and depression as a teenager and found that writing gave her emotional release: "Whenever I had a problem that I couldn't talk about, I would just come to the typewriter, cry, and then type and type and type. And it would leave me."

She discovered a focus for her writing when she visited with the pioneers of her area and listened to their stories. "It was like opening the history book of southern Alberta. Their tales were fascinating," she said. "They enriched my life." Preserving their stories became Irene's mission.

In 1934, when she was twenty, she married rancher David McCaugherty. They spent five years on his parents' ranch near the Oldman River, west of Lethbridge, then moved with their son, Ron, to an area near Stavely in the picturesque Porcupine Hills of south-western Alberta. There they established a mixed farming operation.

As a couple, they lived in two different worlds, according to Irene. David lived in the workaday world of livestock auctions and chicken and hog sales. Irene "walked the hills of loneliness seeking the key to my freedom." She eventually found it in the talents God gave her. "I could draw and write. These were my gifts to share. God had offered me a job to enlighten the hearts of others."

Her first article, published in the *Lethbridge Herald* in 1952, led to a series of columns for the newspaper that she called *Diary of a Farmer's Wife*. She wrote for the *Family Herald* in Montreal and also for *Country Guide* and *Canadian Cattleman*.

In her columns Irene documented the joys and hardships of pioneer life. She interviewed the pioneers whose stories she had heard as a child and told her readers how "their roots were transplanted in the new frontier of western Canada." "They had faith in their dreams," she said. "I am grateful to these people."

With money saved from her writing endeavours, Irene bought herself a camera. "I went to every branding I heard of and followed all the rodeos," she said. "I was trigger-happy with a camera. I loved working with it." Her photography led in turn to painting, which she regarded as just another form of storytelling. "I guess I lived more in the past than in the present," she said. "With the painting, I could create historical recordings—stories of ranch life, farmers, and old-timers." She painted on wide-screen strips of canvas, twenty-two inches wide by eight inches deep, "simply developed from years of viewing ranch life through the windshield of a truck."

One of her first commissions was a mural for a Lethbridge tavern, and from there she moved into the upscale world of art galleries and curated exhibitions. Broader recognition followed. Critics compared her to Grandma Moses, the farmer's wife who painted naive and colourful scenes of rural American life.

Irene ran an art and souvenir shop in Fort Macleod during the late 1960s and early 1970s but she found that the business took her away too much from what she really wanted to do—paint and write. "I was an artist and writer suffering from malnutrition until God offered me a job." She sold the shop and began spending more time at the old school desk in her acreage home that doubled as a type-writer table and easel.

Each of Irene's paintings mirrored a tiny segment of rural Alberta life. Her subjects included country dances, cattle roundups, corn roasts, fairs, and rodeos. "While I painted pictures portraying your lifestyle, you dramatized the action," she wrote in a poem dedicated to her husband.

David McCaugherty died in 1981 after forty-seven years of marriage. In her poem Irene thanked him "for the lifestyle that enriched my years. My marriage taught me to face the odds and win."

Her husband's death caused her to write poems suffused with nostalgia. "My loneliness influenced the thoughts in my head." With her writing and painting, she hoped to "reach some other lonely person and perhaps make them smile." Central to this was finding a way of dealing with her loneliness. "I wrote many spiritual thoughts and took comfort in the beauty of nature."

Irene eventually left her acreage and moved into Fort Macleod. In 1993 she was diagnosed with breast cancer. She joked about it after undergoing radiation treatment in Calgary. "I figured if it took me seventy-eight years to get one lump, well, maybe I'd be all right for another seventy-eight." She continued to write and paint even as her energy level dropped. "As one comes face to face with a problem, we can either wither, submit to fear [and] the unknown, or we can accept the challenge to cope."

She self-published two books after her diagnosis. *The Ladders We Climb* (1994) is a collection of poems, drawings, and stories that reflect her life. *I Just Couldn't Say Goodbye and Shadows of the Past* (1995) combines two collections of poems. One recalls old friends whose "spiritual strength calmed the road of my journey." The other is dedicated to family members and pioneers who inspired her.

In 1995 the University of Lethbridge awarded Irene an honorary laws doctorate for her contribution to Alberta history, which includes a group of thirty paintings that she created to commemorate Lethbridge's centennial in 1985. She considered the degree quite an honour, especially since her formal schooling had ended after Grade six. A permanent exhibition of her paintings was installed in the Sir Alexander Galt Museum in Lethbridge, and compilations of her writings, photography, and paintings have formed the basis of history videos for southern Alberta schools.

Irene wrote and painted until a month before she died, a few days short of her eighty-second birthday, in November 1996. It was her goal, she said, to continue capturing and preserving the history of the Canadian West as long as she had breath in her body. She wanted to do it especially for her grandchildren and great-grandchildren. "I'd like to make them proud that they are Canadian," she said. "If they know the roots of their heritage, they have something to be proud of."

W.O. Mitchell

Author and performer

1914–1998

Author Rudy Wiebe said it first and said it best. W.O. Mitchell, he said, was "Canada's most marvellous word spinner." Mitchell "spun" these words in the first sentence of his first book, *Who Has Seen the Wind*: "Here was the least common denominator of nature, the skeleton requirements simply, of land and sky—Saskatchewan prairie."

With those opening words, William Ormond Mitchell began a relationship with Canadians that lasted more than half a century and made him the country's most beloved storyteller. *Who Has Seen the Wind*, published in 1947 when Mitchell was thirty-three, remains the great Canadian novel of boyhood and the country's most evocative literary treatment of the Prairies and its people. It tells about a young boy's coming of age in a small town on the Saskatchewan prairie, and reflects a view of the Prairies as a landscape with its own terrible beauty. Because his father died when he was a boy, Mitchell was able to sympathetically portray a child's struggle to understand mortality in a place where the wind becomes a symbol for God.

Mitchell was both a serious writer and an entertainer, a disciplined literary craftsman and a limelight-loving performer. He was a ham actor at heart, he said, who had harboured ambitions of working in the theatre. He took elocution lessons to overcome his shyness and discovered that like his Irish father, who was both a druggist and a professional declaimer of verse, W.O. had the gift of the public gab. In the early 1930s, he studied playwriting at the University of Washington, then spent three years in Seattle writing plays and acting with a repertory company called the Penthouse Players.

Mitchell thrived on being the centre of attention. "But in my generation, there was really no chance to go on stage in this country," he said. "There was only the CBC Radio stage." He abandoned his theatrical ambitions for a while and began writing for the CBC. His more than three hundred scripts of *Jake and the Kid*, broadcast between 1950 and 1958, brought Mitchell's words to thousands of listeners who might never read his novels.

His radio work eventually returned him to his first love, writing for the theatre. In 1976 Theatre Calgary presented a stage version of his radio play *Back to Beulah*. A precursor to Ken Kesey's 1962 novel, *One Flew Over the Cuckoo's Nest*, *Beulah* tells the story of three residents of a mental institution who riot while undergoing experimental psychiatric treatment. The play transferred to Toronto and won the 1976 Chalmers Play Award for distinguished contribution to theatre in Canada. Mitchell told the awards audience he wished he could start over in Canadian theatre because it was expanding so rapidly.

Theatre Calgary's artistic director, Rick McNair, took Mitchell at his word. He asked the author what else he had in his satchel besides *Back to Beulah*. It turned out that Mitchell had plenty.

The first play was *The Black Bonspiel of Wullie MacCrimmon*, a Faustian whimsy about a Presbyterian shoemaker who stakes his soul in a curling match with the devil. It made its Calgary stage debut in 1979, after a summer festival production in Peterborough, Ontario, and immediately promised to become one of the most popular Canadian plays ever seen on the local stage. Theatre Calgary revived it twice, and the play made a further encore appearance in 1997 at Alberta Theatre Projects to coincide with the Labatt's Brier in Calgary.

Mitchell's next hit at Theatre Calgary was *The Kite*, a 1981 play about a 117-year-old curmudgeon who wants his epitaph to read "Gone—by God." It was revived at Theatre Calgary during the 1992 season and reaffirmed Mitchell's popularity as a theatre folk humourist.

The old ham actor also had an opportunity to strut the boards himself. He loved to perform his work—he was often compared to Stephen Leacock and Mark Twain—and his public readings, presented as *An Evening with W.O. Mitchell*, were sellout successes. Though he sometimes complained about being stereotyped as "this corncob humourist from the Prairies," Mitchell reinforced the image in his public performances, revelling in the speech patterns and idioms of his characters. Even off the stage, he could hardly refrain from playing the folksy humourist and cracker-barrel philosopher. "He loved to perform before an audience and needed that feedback," his daughter Barbara told a Toronto magazine. Mitchell's son Ormond said, "The meals at our house were very loud and lively." Publisher Douglas Gibson, Mitchell's longtime friend and editor, recalled a meal with the author at a Toronto hotel when the maitre d' had no choice but to ask Mitchell to tone down his raucous impersonation of an evangelical preacher in full fury.

His public performances eventually overshadowed anything he did as a writer. "*Who Has Seen the Wind* cast a long shadow," wrote Saskatchewan author Sharon Butala. "Although many of his novels were commercial successes, it is probably an accurate judgment that he never again achieved the brilliance of his first novel." Gibson said Mitchell suffered the "terrible fate" of having his first novel become a spectacular success, "and he spent the rest of his writing life with *Who Has Seen the Wind* looking over his shoulder."

Though most associated with Saskatchewan, Mitchell did not spend much time in his native province. He spent his adolescence in Florida, fighting off a case of tuberculosis, and after earning a degree at the University of Alberta, he lived most of the rest of his life close to the Alberta foothills, in High River off and on for twenty years and then in Calgary.

Mitchell died at his Calgary home in February 1998 at age eighty-three after struggling with cancer for five years. He made his last public appearance in June 1996, at the Writers Union of Canada annual meeting, where he told the audience that he had learned at a very young age—both from his father's death, and from seeing gophers killed on the Prairies—that he was mortal. "I guess that time you learn you're going to die is the time you really understand you're human," he said. "Humans must comfort each other, and defend each other against the terror of being human." Pierre Berton, who was in the audience, was moved to tears. "W.O. Mitchell is what I call an original," Berton once wrote. "There is only one of him and there aren't going to be any more."

Jean Hoare

Restaurateur and cookbook author

1914–2000

When Jean Hoare put her Claresholm restaurant up for sale in 1974, she didn't have to do any advertising. Newspapers across Canada did it for her, publishing stories that amounted to free ads. "For sale: rustic restaurant, airport location," said the headline in the *Globe and Mail.* Such was the renown of this country cook, who never took a formal cooking lesson and daringly called herself "the Hoare who cooks," that her every move was big news.

Hoare didn't have to advertise, either, during the twenty years she ran the restaurant, first as a dining room for friends and neighbours at her ranch near Claresholm, north of Lethbridge, and later in what used to be an army service corps storage depot at Claresholm's Second World War airfield. She didn't have to advertise because word just got around.

Her recipe for success was deceptively simple: Serve good food and lots of it. At the Flying N restaurant—so named because of its airport location—every meal was like Sunday dinner at grandma's place. Customers were advised not to eat breakfast—much less lunch—before gorging themselves on the hearty seven-course meals that were Hoare's trademark.

Cooking big meals was something Hoare had done since childhood. At age ten, growing up in Toronto, she was encouraged by her mother to help cook Sunday dinner for the extended family. Hoare would study the recipes and the photographs of plate servings in the *Ladies Home Journal* and serve meals for up to twenty people. It seemed a natural progression to go from that to later serving meals for two hundred people at the Flying N. If she could do it for twenty people who didn't pay, she said, why not for two hundred who did?

Childhood family drives through rural Ontario also influenced Hoare's culinary future. Signs saying "Chicken Dinners Served Sundays" seemed to point in the direction her life would eventually take. Country cooking would always conjure up memories for her of thick cream, hot bread, and lots of butter.

In her twenties, she worked at the Bay department store in Toronto, where colleagues talked about the fabulous meals served at the Marigold Hotel in Niagara Falls, New York. Hoare went down to see for herself and came home with something special—a cookbook containing recipes for all the popular dishes served at the Marigold. Decades later that same cookbook, much thumbed and tattered, was the culinary bible of the Flying N.

Jean moved to southern Alberta during the Second World War to live on a cousin's ranch while her husband, Stan, served overseas with the air force. After the war, she and Stan opted not to return to Ontario. They bought a 375-acre spread near Pulteney, a tiny hamlet about seventy miles south of Calgary.

Raising a son and daughter and cooking for large groups of people became the focus of Hoare's life. She combined her love of cooking with an interest in local history, putting on big barbecues at which she and her neighbours socialized, listened to the tales of the old-timers, and ate their fill. Those gatherings gave birth to the Willow Creek Historical Society, for which Hoare served as recording secretary.

During the 1950s, Hoare's marriage dissolved. To support her two children, she turned their home on the range into a restaurant that she named the Driftwillow. She moved the furniture out of the living room, put in large oak tables that she had bought at auctions for twenty-five dollars each, added seating for forty people, and told her neighbours she was open for wedding banquets, birthday parties, and anniversary celebrations.

Her first customers, and her staff, were her neighbours. They took reservations on the party-line telephone whenever Hoare was busy, and they showed up to help her when they knew a crowd was coming in.

The restaurant didn't make much money in the beginning, so Hoare worked for the Willow Creek municipal district as secretary-treasurer to augment her income.

Business began to pick up after a roving Calgary newspaper columnist named Ken Liddell wrote a story about "the lady in the country who cooks." Customers came from all parts of southern Alberta to sample her roast beef and sourdough bread. She put a map of Alberta on the wall and asked customers to stick coloured pins in it to indicate their home towns.

By the mid-1960s, a map of Canada had replaced the map of Alberta, and the Driftwillow had become too small to handle the growing volume of customers who wanted to try Jean's beef and bread.

Water also became a problem. The well couldn't handle the volume of customers who wanted to use the toilets every night. A sign on the washroom door said, "Don't Flush Unless Absolutely Necessary."

To expand her restaurant, Hoare sold 160 acres and bought the old supply depot at the Claresholm industrial airport. The building, which she decorated in what she called "depression western," could accommodate five times as many customers. The airport location proved to be an attraction for private pilots from Montana, Idaho, and other parts of the United States. Hoare replaced the map of Canada with a map of North America.

In 1971 and for three years after that, the Flying N was listed in Anne Hardy's *Where To Eat In Canada* as one of the country's top ten restaurants. The publicity, said Hoare, just about did her in. It attracted more guests than her two-hundred-seat facility could handle, and those who arrived without reservations were invariably doomed to disappointment.

Comics Wayne and Shuster were two of the celebrity guests who made it to Claresholm to eat at the Flying N. They left an autographed picture that read: "To Jean of the Flying N from Johnny Wayne, the lazy W, and Frank Shuster, the smart S."

By 1974, when her staff had grown from a handful of neighbours to a payroll of thirty, the shine had worn off. Hoare's health began to fail, and she envisaged herself and the restaurant going down together. She sold out in 1975 but unwisely provided the buyer with a second mortgage, interest-free for five years.

Four years later, at age sixty-five, the bankers asked her to take over the restaurant as receiver/manager while they looked for another buyer. The first buyer had amassed a terminal debt load and fled town. Hoare's excessively generous sale agreement had cost her about $150,000 that was meant for a comfortable retirement.

In early 1982 Hoare parted company with the Flying N for the last time. High interest rates had discouraged potential purchasers. She held a farewell party for her friends and talked about spending her retirement writing a cookbook sprinkled with anecdotal reminiscences.

Two years later the book became a reality. Jean published *The Best Little Cookbook in the West* with help, advice, and financial backing from Calgary author Nancy Millar. "She had such life force, such willingness to get involved," wrote Millar in the *Globe and Mail*.

The book sold fifteen thousand copies in its first printing, and Hoare, at age sixty-nine, embarked on a new career as a celebrity author. She did forty-eight half-hour cooking shows for Calgary's CFAC television, made guest appearances on national talk shows, and was introduced in the Alberta legislature by Macleod legislator Leroy Fjordbotten. She wondered whimsically if her book would make the *Guinness Book of World Records* as the first cookbook mentioned in the *Hansard*.

Her second book, *Jean's Beans,* also did well, and her weekly column, *Driftwillow Diary,* published in the local newspaper in Vulcan, was popular.

By the time Hoare wrote her final column, at the end of 1996, her writing was appearing in the weekly papers in Okotoks, Nanton, Claresholm, and High River, as well as in Vulcan. "The happy memories overshadow any regrets," she wrote in her last column. The eighty-two-year-old quipped, "If I had known I was going to live so long, I would have taken better care of myself."

Jean was eighty-five when she died of a heart attack in January 2000 at her Driftwillow Ranch home. It's said she died at her kitchen table while eating a cookie. "How very appropriate," wrote Nancy Millar in an obituary story in the *Globe and Mail*. At the height of the Flying N's success, when most of her customers came from far-away places, Jean used to say tongue-in-cheek that her epitaph should read, "I've come all the way from Calgary." More appropriately now, it should read, "She made a big reputation with a little restaurant that grew up and became famous."

Father Pat O'Byrne

Priest and poverty activist

1915–1996

Father Pat O'Byrne worked among the poor when he was studying for the priesthood in Toronto during the 1930s. He was still working among the poor when in his late seventies. Physically handicapped but still mobile, he travelled around Calgary's Beltline district in a motorized wheelchair, dispensing blessings and words of comfort. Nothing could stop this man from doing God's work, noted a religion writer for the *Calgary Herald,* "not even a ticket to heaven."

For Father Pat, giving handouts to the poor was never enough. While he did his fair share of giving, providing food, clothing, and shelter where needed, he also attacked the root causes of poverty. "You have to work at it," he said, "to improve the conditions that lead to welfare, unemployment, and food bank lineups."

The son of a Calgary hardware store owner, Father Pat was the fourth priest from Calgary to be ordained in his home town during the first twenty-seven years of the Calgary Roman Catholic diocese. His ordination made headlines in the local papers in 1940. Seven years later, Father Pat moved to Claresholm, where he served as parish administrator and pastor for ten years, and started an adults-in-training program for Catholic youth that spread into a national movement.

Father Pat returned to Calgary in 1957, and over the next two decades he took on a series of assignments with various Catholic social agencies, including Diocesan Charities, Catholic Family Service, and the Catholic Council on Social Affairs.

Because poverty knows no denominational boundaries, it was perhaps inevitable that his work would eventually lead to an alliance between the social agencies of the various churches in Calgary. During the 1960s, Father Pat teamed with Calgary rabbi Lewis Ginsburg and a group of Protestant ministers to start the Calgary

Inter-Faith Community Action Association, a group that established the first food bank in Calgary and the first drop-in centre.

The inter-faith group provided Father Pat with the perfect vehicle for turning into action his belief that churches should focus on what they have in common—and set aside their denominational differences—when they help those on the margins of society. In Rabbi Ginsburg, he found a perfect partner for his social justice initiatives.

Ginsburg was quite a colourful character. He claimed to be the first rabbi in Calgary, maybe even the first in Canada, to climb into a ring and take on a wrestling opponent in the name of church and charity. He also claimed to be the only rabbi ever to become an honorary colonel in the Salvation Army.

Ginsburg became, in the words of a friend, "one of the great men who helped Father Pat survive himself." When Father Pat announced in 1971 that he was going to become the first Roman Catholic priest in English Canada to try for a seat in the provincial legislature, his fellow priests looked the other way. But Ginsburg stood behind him, serving as public relations consultant.

Father Pat, running on the Social Credit ticket, eventually lost to Conservative Merv Leitch in the election that swept Peter Lougheed's Tories to power. He put his Roman collar back on, declared that he was through with politics, and said that he and Rabbi Ginsburg were going to take their inter-faith show on the road. They manned Salvation Army kettles together in the Bay department store at Christmastime, jokingly debated the respective charms of Hanukkah and Christmas at Rotary Club luncheons, and co-hosted a cable television show called *The Big Ten,* referring to the Ten Commandments observed by the Jewish and Christian faiths.

Most of Father Pat's public shenanigans with Ginsburg were done in a spirit of fun, but they did have a serious underlying purpose. "If I have any message to Christians and Jews, it is 'let's get behind those Vietnamese in the boats,'" Father Pat once told a B'nai B'rith meeting. Afterwards, someone noticed him walking away from the House of Israel with a golden yarmulke still on his head. "A man wearing a clerical collar and a Jewish skullcap seemed a fitting tribute to the ecumenical ideals of Inter-Faith," said the observer.

Former Solicitor General Roy Farran described Father Pat as "a man with a twinkle in his eye, a contempt for pomposity, and a certain love for the unorthodox." During the early 1980s, Father Pat shocked friends when he told a reporter he was considering leaving the priesthood for reasons that he would not make public. But he quickly changed his mind when he realized the resignation would simply be disregarded by the thousands of Calgarians who had known and loved him for more than forty years. To them, he would always be Father Pat.

He died in a Calgary nursing home at age eighty-one in May 1996, more than two years after the death of his old pal Rabbi Ginsburg. He had served as a priest for fifty-six years, and his ticket to heaven had finally arrived. A fellow cleric called Father Pat "one of those rare people able to walk with kings and humble people." Another said, "Everything for him was an opportunity to touch the lives of people that others would ignore." Father Pat's younger brother, former Calgary bishop Paul O'Byrne, said he "just wore out." He wore out trying to turn Calgary into a community where people respect one another and look after one another, regardless of creed, colour, or economic circumstances.

Jack Gallagher

Geologist and industrialist

1916–1998

The petroleum industry, which Albertans call the "oilpatch," has always attracted gamblers who refuse to become mired in the swamp of the status quo. When others say, "It can't be done," the entrepreneurs who embody the "can-do" spirit of the oilpatch say, "Let's try it."

Jack Gallagher was typical of this entrepreneurial breed. He spent a lifetime convincing people with money to finance his quest for oil in parts of the world where oil had never been found. During the 1940s he ventured into South American jungles and North African deserts, hunting oil for Shell and Standard Oil of New Jersey. During the 1950s, he looked northward toward the Canadian Arctic and saw "one, maybe two Middle Easts" in the Beaufort Sea. Nobody else could see so much as a thimbleful of oil there, but Gallagher had a vision.

A market gardener's son from Winnipeg, Gallagher earned a degree in geology at the University of Manitoba, then began his life as an adventurer and explorer. His fascination with the north started in the 1930s, when he worked for the Geological Survey of Canada as a twenty-year-old student geologist. The northern wilderness left a lasting impression on him. "The great thrill was that you were opening up country white men hadn't seen before," he said.

Then came what Gallagher called his apprentice years, when he travelled the world as an oil explorer for Shell and Standard Oil. For much of that time, he seemed to be writing the script for future movies starring the fictional adventurer-geologist Indiana Jones. In Peru, Gallagher persuaded unfriendly Andean tribesman to guide him safely through the headwaters of the Amazon. On a return visit, he avoided certain death by steering his truck into the side of a cliff after his driver fainted and the vehicle swerved toward the edge of a mountain precipice. Gallagher worked in pain for a year after that incident before learning from a doctor that he had fractured three vertebrae.

In 1950 Gallagher left Standard to accept an intriguing offer from the American owners of Ontario-based Dome Mines. The owners wanted him to help them diversify into oil and tap into some of the wealth being generated following the big oil discoveries in Leduc and Redwater. The decision for Gallagher was easy. He had fallen in love with Calgary after just one visit. At age thirty-three, he became the first employee of an unknown Calgary company called Dome Exploration.

Because his mining bosses knew nothing about oil, Gallagher was able to make all his own calls. He made them well, starting with promising discoveries of oil at Drumheller and gas at Provost. But his real interest lay in the area north of the Mackenzie River delta. Over the next twenty-five years, Dome spent hundreds of millions of dollars drilling in the Beaufort Sea. It built a corporate fleet to rival the tonnage of Canada's navy and occupied a land position comparable to the original charter of the Hudson's Bay Company.

With his ineffable charm—the media dubbed him "Smiling Jack Gallagher"—the persuasive oilman sold his vision of the Beaufort to bankers and government without ever providing any tangible return to justify such major expenditures. "What's most astonishing about Jack Gallagher," wrote author Peter C. Newman, "is that all his power and all his glory have been achieved without Dome hunting down a single elephant-size oil discovery."

This might have suggested that Dome's arctic adventure was nothing but smoke and mirrors. But investors believed in Dome because they saw their shares multiply 315-fold over a twenty-seven-year period. Author Jim Lyon reported in *Dome: The Rise and Fall of the House that Jack Built*, that a block of one hundred Dome shares purchased for $380 in 1954 was worth $120,000 by 1981.

Then came the crash. In 1982 the house that Jack built collapsed under the weight of a crushing $7.03-billion debt, caused by the ill-fated takeover of Hudson's Bay Oil and Gas. Dome's most important corporate activity at that point had been acquisition. Under Bill Richards, the lawyer who was Gallagher's second-in-command, Dome invested money in Siebens Oil and Gas, Kaiser Resources, and

TransCanada Pipelines, and went after Hudson's Bay Oil and Gas just before interest rates soared to twenty-three percent, oil prices dropped, and demand for oil slackened.

If Dome had declared bankruptcy then, the loss could have brought down one, and possibly two, major Canadian banks. Gallagher's personal loss, scarcely without equal in Canadian financial history, was estimated at more than $118 million. He resigned, along with company president Richards, and Dome was sold to Amoco for $5.5 billion.

Leaving Dome was tough for Gallagher. "It hurts," he said. "I gave the company the best years of my life." But he did not betray his hurt in his farewell speech. Author Lyon described it as "quietly gracious, upbeat, and optimistic, and—in the circumstances—totally unexpected." A bank official called it "a class act."

Was the discovery of oil in the Beaufort an impossible dream? Not according to the Gulf Canada exploration people, who in 1985 turned Gallagher's northern dream into reality with a sizeable oil find. The discovery was not quite large enough to warrant the expense of developing it, but Gallagher was gratified when a Gulf vice president phoned him and said, "We know if it hadn't been for you, we wouldn't be here." All great geologists are true believers.

Gallagher moved on to other ventures. He founded Pauma Petroleum, naming it after the California valley where he wintered with wife, Katie. He jogged and skied and gave to causes he considered worthy. His interest in diet and fitness inspired a low-calorie turkey sandwich lunch called the Gallagher Special that was served at the Petroleum Club. He supported the Reform Party with money and speeches. He started an educational foundation to help teachers adapt to new technology in the classroom. He gave money to a Calgary hospice, where he eventually died after a nine-year battle with cancer.

Gallagher died in December 1998 at age eighty-two. During the last years of his life, he hadn't been a leading player in the oilpatch. But his influence was not forgotten. Every time a new discovery was made in the Beaufort, someone would remember that Smiling Jack Gallagher had been the first to talk about a frozen Middle East in the Canadian Arctic, bursting with 90 million barrels of oil and other riches.

To the last, Gallagher remained a breaker of new ground. Education and Reform Party politics became his prime interests as his involvement in the oilpatch declined. "You only go through life once," he said, "and it's a lot more fun if you plough a different furrow, rather than the same furrow that everybody else has ploughed."

William Morrow

Judge

1917–1980

Justice William Morrow will be remembered mainly for the ten years he spent in the Northwest Territories trying to make the white man's law of Canada's south work for the indigenous peoples of the north. But he should also be remembered for the bookends of his legal career. Morrow started out in Edmonton in the 1940s, when enough oil was gushing from the ground to make a new millionaire every week. He ended his career in Calgary during the 1970s, when there was so much commercial construction going on that the crane was said jokingly to be the city's official bird.

Morrow started in law as a junior partner to his father, a Manitoba-born lawyer of Irish ancestry who had pitched a tent along the North Saskatchewan River to save money while studying law at the University of Alberta before the First World War. Morrow started practising with his father in 1940, then took time out to serve in the navy during the Second World War. He returned to Edmonton in 1945, and after losing eleven cases in two weeks, he began to wonder if he should have stayed in the navy. He even wrote to naval authorities in Ottawa "asking if they would take me back without loss of seniority." Then two of Morrow's losses were overturned on appeal, and the young lawyer was on his way to building a successful legal career.

Some of his cases made legal history. In 1950, appearing on behalf of two Redwater farmers, he argued successfully before the Supreme Court of Canada that the mineral rights granted to oil companies should be restricted to the oil under the ground, and not apply to the sand and gravel on the surface. In 1959 he was involved in the last case from Canada to be taken on appeal to the Privy Council in England. Morrow lost the case, which involved defending the owner of a petroleum lease against a lawsuit filed by a drilling company that hadn't been paid for its services. "At least," said Morrow, "I did arrive at the foot of the throne in my search for justice."

Morrow's northern odyssey began in 1960, when Justice Jack Sissons, the first judge of the territorial court of the Northwest Territories, asked him to act as a volunteer defence counsel in cases in which the defendants had no legal representation. Morrow accepted the assignment without hesitation. As a boy, he had loved the novels of G.A. Henty, "great historical adventure stories written to inspire young men to seek service in the cause of country and empire. Those books had a profound effect on me and created a desire to seek my own adventures." He had promised himself that one day, when he felt the forces of fate drifting directly into his path, he would seize the moment and create his own story. That day occurred when Justice Sissons offered his invitation to work in the north.

Morrow spent six years travelling the northern circuit by aircraft and dogsled then took over from Sissons as chief justice. The stories of his northern adventures are the stuff of legend. He flew more than sixty-four thousand kilometres a year, taking "justice to every man's door," armed with a twenty-two-calibre pistol, a hunting knife, and a case of rye whisky. The pistol and the knife were part of his survival kit for the lonely flights over glaciers and barren lands. The whisky was a gift for the people in remote communities who put him up for the night. He used the gun for target practice whenever his plane was grounded for repairs, and often told his pilot to put the aircraft down near a lake or river when he felt like spending an afternoon fishing. Though he came from the south, it didn't take Morrow long to adapt to the ways of the north.

Because people in the remote communities could not come to court, Judge Morrow brought the court to them, in improvised courtrooms. He once interviewed a defendant in the only room where he could be assured privacy—the outhouse. He also heard cases in schoolrooms, amid the litter left by elementary students. He even used his plane's cabin as a makeshift courtroom.

But Morrow was more than just a judge who dispensed homespun frontier justice. He was also a maker of landmark decisions that will affect the lives of northerners for years to come. His legacy includes a sentencing strategy that took into account the shorter life expectancy of northern peoples, greater tolerance of aboriginal values in interpreting the law, and the creation of juries composed of men and women from the community of the accused.

His most famous decision involved a man charged under the Indian Act for being drunk off reserve land, in the lobby of a Yellowknife hotel. If the man, Joseph Drybones, had been white, he could have been charged under a liquor ordinance that carried a lesser penalty. Morrow ruled that the Indian Act contravened the "equality before the law" clause of the Canadian Bill of Rights because its scope and penalty differed from that governing other Canadians. The Crown appealed his verdict, but the Supreme Court of Canada—in a divided judgment that some people called the decision of the century—upheld the Morrow decision.

Morrow completed his last arctic circuit among the Native communities of the Northwest Territories in the spring of 1976. Some wondered why he seemed to be abandoning the people he had come to love. "Why was he leaving the best friends he would ever know, and ignoring the mystical call of the north?" his son Will asks in the introduction to *Northern Justice: The Memoirs of Mr. Justice William G. Morrow.* "The truth was that my father was a weary man. A decade of combating not only the northern elements, but the insensitivity of Ottawa politicians, had taken a toll on the man who had dreamed as a boy of enjoying a life of great adventure."

Morrow accepted a seat on the Alberta Supreme Court after leaving the Northwest Territories, and he served in the appellate division in Calgary until his sudden death in August 1980. He was sixty-three years old and had suffered from heart disease. His son edited his memoirs and had them published in 1995. Reflecting on his career as a lawyer and judge, Morrow wrote that common sense had always been his guiding principle. He looked for the common sense answer ("often preferable to the 'just' answer") and then "found some law to support it." If this meant that he had to "bend the law a little at times," so be it. Northern justice, he said, was never about precedents. It was about "bringing the law and justice as close together as possible."

Betty O'Hanlon

Adventurer

1918–1993

"You can't go to war, you're a girl," people told Betty Gilliatt in 1941, when she talked about joining the Canadian army and volunteering for service overseas. They might also have said that she couldn't become a treasure hunter, a gunrunner, or a wildcatter. But she did all of the above and more. Life for Betty was always a great adventure.

The adventure began with her birth in Newfoundland in 1918, more than thirty years before residents of the island province voted to join Confederation. Her father worked as chief engineer for the Dominion Steel and Coal Company. Her mother was a schoolteacher from Nova Scotia. Betty studied at home under her mother's tutelage up to Grade five, then went to boarding school in St. John's. In her final year, she was given the school award for "best all-around girl." She didn't think she deserved it. "As I was to find out years later in the army, awards were given not so much for good behaviour as for undetected crime."

In 1937 Betty left for Dalhousie University in Halifax to earn a science degree in biology. She specialized in bacteriology, graduated in the spring of 1941, and went to work as a technician at the public health laboratory in St. John's.

Her friends at university were right when they said she couldn't go to war. The Canadian Women's Army Corps hadn't been formed yet. But its formation later that year gave Betty her opportunity. She enlisted with the hope she might be sent to England as an ambulance driver. "With your training?" people said. "Don't be silly." However, when she was commissioned as a second lieutenant in the Medical Corps, she was told she had a chance to go overseas.

In 1944, while stationed at Camp Borden, she met and married Harry O'Hanlon, a twenty-eight-year-old lieutenant with the Canadian Armoured Corps. Born in Edmonton, Harry had become part of the reclusive Mannix family when his father died in an automobile accident and his mother married Fred S. Mannix, the Manitoba-born construction pioneer who made a fortune building hydroelectric dams in Alberta. Harry was in Panama, working for the canal company, when the Second World War broke out. He enlisted in the Canadian army and headed to Europe.

Army regulations prohibited married women from going overseas, but Betty made it onto the boat because her Defence Department bosses mistakenly thought her job description applied to a man. She achieved another army first when she was subsequently posted to a military hospital in Normandy. She became the only married woman to serve in a European combat zone during the Second World War. "I never wanted equality with men," she quipped. "I am satisfied with being superior."

When the war was over, most Canadian soldiers talked about returning home and picking up where they had left off. Betty and Harry, however, wanted to look for treasure in Central America. They had heard of pirate gold—the so-called "loot of Lima"—being buried on a Pacific island administered by Costa Rica, and they thought that searching for it would help them forget the horrors of war. But after two fruitless expeditions to Cocos Island, they abandoned treasure hunting for other adventures.

The O'Hanlons became briefly involved in gun-running when a group of Panamanian revolutionaries offered them $5,000 for the use of their boat to smuggle guns from Costa Rica into Panama. The revolutionaries were trying to reinstate an ousted Panamanian president who had been removed from elected office by a military dictator. Betty and Harry never received their promised pay, but they became internationally notorious after the incident, which *Time* magazine described as "unemployed treasure hunters staging a comic opera revolution in Central America."

Betty and Harry eventually traded their quest for yellow gold for the hunt for black gold. After hearing about the big oil finds up north, they moved back to Alberta in 1949. Several years later they were on the road again when wildcatting Harry struck oil in northern Montana. They lived in Cut Bank for seven years before deciding, in 1961, that what they really wanted was a farm of their own in the foothills southwest of Calgary.

They bought a farm west of High River and threw themselves wholeheartedly into their next adventure, running the Canadian branch of the Maharishi Mahesh Yogi's International Meditation Society. This adventure was to take them twice to India, where Betty finally found spiritual peace.

Harry, meanwhile, found he had a talent for sculpting. By the mid-1980s, his bronze statues of horses and Natives were selling internationally to museums and private collectors. In 1989 his *Family of Horses* sculpture became a permanent fixture on the plaza in front of Calgary's city hall. The same year, Betty documented the story of her life with Harry in an autobiography entitled *Finding a Familiar Stranger.* She described her husband as "my friend and companion in the great adventure of life," and said that she had found in southern India a place that was "truly the home of our hearts, no matter where fate willed our bodies to live."

Fate willed that she spend her last years in Red Deer Lake. She died of cancer in June 1993 at age seventy-five. Harry, then seventy-seven, was devastated, but took some consolation from their shared spiritual belief that all is eternal and that "nothing whatever is born, and nothing dies, anywhere in the world at any time." He immersed himself in his sculpting. With the encouragement of a friend, he completed a bronze that is now displayed at the Calgary International Airport. He also did a commissioned work for the RCMP. A copy of his *Family of Horses* sculpture went on display at the Spruce Meadows showjumping facility, and a miniature was given to Queen Elizabeth during a royal visit to Calgary.

Harry died in March 1996 at age eighty. Friends said his life had become a chore as he struggled to find his way without Betty, his closest friend, fellow traveller, and life's companion of more than fifty years. He asked that no funeral service be held. "Please only remember me as I was on this earth."

Webster Macdonald Sr.

Maverick lawyer

1918–1995

Webster Macdonald Sr. was a spiritual descendant of the mavericks and renegades who populated the West during the 1880s. His forebears openly defied Prohibition and gambling laws and supported the Metis during the North-West Rebellion. Macdonald, working as a criminal lawyer in Calgary during the 1950s, defied convention by taking on cases that nobody else would touch.

He called himself "the champion of the underprivileged and defender of the damned."

His first case in Calgary involved a man charged with shooting a horse that had kicked in the door of his truck. His last case, in 1990, saw Macdonald representing a Calgary screenwriter who claimed to have created the Ewok characters that appeared in the movie *Return of the Jedi*. In between, Macdonald advocated for a succession of colourful defendants. The more bizarre the case, it seemed, the more likely that Macdonald would be involved in it.

Sometimes he won his cases with arguments that other lawyers would find outrageous. He won an acquittal for the man who shot the horse, for instance, by noting that the animal had only one testicle. "A horse with one ball is nasty and ill-tempered and deserves to be shot," said Macdonald. The judge agreed and dismissed the charge.

Macdonald came to Calgary in 1957 after serving as a Crown prosecutor in his home town of Kentville, Nova Scotia. In 1956 Robert Stanfield's Tories ended the long Liberal reign in Nova Scotia and, according to local custom, all federal appointments were immediately transferred to Tory supporters. Finding himself unemployed, Macdonald headed west with his wife, formerly Lieutenant Sheilah Florance of the Women's Royal Canadian Naval Service, the first two of their five sons, and their dog.

A short stint with Standard Oil in Calgary convinced Macdonald to open his own practice. He opened what he called his "people in trouble" office in a small house that had previously belonged to two popular homeopaths who laced their remedies with gin. Those were the days, said Macdonald, when Calgary had no more than two restaurants of any distinction. But the city was about to grow.

Macdonald added the "Sr." to his name during the early 1970s, when his son Webster Jr. began practising in the Calgary criminal justice system. He described his son as "an establishment lawyer." He considered himself nonestablishment or, at the very least, unconventional. He declared his maverick status in 1961, when he successfully defended a Calgary woman charged in the stabbing death of her husband's mistress. Macdonald won the case by convincing the jury that the husband, an army corporal, was a "repulsive reptile."

In 1963 Macdonald got into trouble with the legal establishment when he took on the appeal of a Calgary madam who had been sent to prison for running a brothel near the Stampede grounds. "No one should be sentenced to ten years for simply keeping a cathouse," declared Macdonald. He based his appeal on evidence that the prosecutor had acted indiscreetly by sending roses and thank-you notes to the prostitutes who had testified for the Crown. The legal establishment cried foul, and Macdonald was ostracized.

"I had to pay for my low blow," Macdonald said afterwards. "I was never elected a bencher of the law society, or appointed a QC, and I was never offered to be made a judge." Such was the lot of the professional maverick. "If you commit the great North American crime of daring to be different, you pay the price of not being accepted."

Sometimes not being accepted was only part of the price. The law society twice suspended Macdonald for "unprofessional conduct." He was cited once for criminal contempt and, in 1966, he was charged with forgery and uttering false documents in a land deal. Lawyer Milt Harradence (later an appeal court justice) took the case, and Macdonald was "resoundingly acquitted." And when the case was over, "I sued them all." But, as the lawsuit was against the Crown prosecutor, the police, and a judge, "there was only one problem: I could not find a lawyer in Calgary to take my case." Macdonald said later that the emotional toll was lasting. "I've paid, and paid, and paid."

A few of his cases brought prestige, most notably a landmark cash settlement he won for the Treaty Seven Indians in 1973, when the federal government was forced to honour the promises of Queen Victoria and pay the Natives money owed to them for almost a century. But it was for his defence of the people on the margins of society that Macdonald will be remembered. One of his more colourful clients was Jimmy the Con, whose record ran to 485 fraud convictions but who ran for mayor of Calgary and collected quite a few votes. Another was a stripper who did anatomically amazing things with peashooters and Ping-Pong balls. For such cases, the *Calgary Herald* dubbed Macdonald the "Perry Mason of Canada." "The more desperate the circumstances, the more damning the evidence, the more Macdonald enjoys coming to the rescue," said the paper. "They fascinated me," Macdonald told the *Herald* shortly before he moved his practice to Saltspring Island, British Columbia, in 1989. "They were so colourful, so outrageous."

His last big case in Calgary involved a $100-million lawsuit against Hollywood producer George Lucas for alleged copyright infringement and breach of implied contract. A Calgary screenwriter, Dean Preston, claimed to have developed the Ewok name and character in a script he mailed to Lucas in 1978. Lucas denied ever receiving the script and insisted that he had created the Ewok name and characters for his 1983 movie, *Return of the Jedi*, the concluding episode of his lucrative *Star Wars* trilogy. Macdonald lost the case on appeal.

The move to Saltspring Island was ostensibly a semi-retirement move for Macdonald after doctors replaced his arthritic knees with plastic-metallic balls. But the lawyer carried with him a briefcase full of strange cases, including a patent application for a man "who invented an engine to take you to the Moon and back on Sunday afternoons." Macdonald also brought his memories and notes for an autobiography he published in 1993 as *Memoirs of a Maverick Lawyer*. "A fun book with a serious message," he called it. "Law is, and always will be, the most exciting game in town."

Macdonald died of an apparent heart attack in August 1995 at age seventy-six. "They did break the mould with you," his family wrote in his obituary. Macdonald's own words provide the coda: "I was always a nonconformist and had a burning desire to help people, no matter how heinous their crime or how hopeless their cause. I was a rebel, a maverick who dared to be different. I was a thorn in the side of the legal establishment, but I was not running a popularity contest, and I'd take on cases other lawyers wouldn't touch, if I felt they had merit and their cause was just. I did it my way, and given my druthers, I'd do it all over again."

Stan Waters

Soldier and Canada's only elected senator

1920–1991

At the end of the day, Stan Waters was remembered as the first and only person in history to gatecrash the Senate without a prime ministerial invitation. He was an inexperienced politician who, at age sixty-nine, brought short-lived democracy to an institution defined by patronage. Were it not for that idiosyncratic late-period stand of man against the state, Waters might be remembered primarily as a war hero. During the Second World War, he served with the famous U.S.-Canadian Devil's Brigade and won a U.S. Silver Star for his role in the liberation of Rome.

He was a parcel of contradictions, this war hero turned politician. Publicly he sang the songs of the Reform Party, but if you listened closely, you would hear a different set of lyrics in private.

He opposed official bilingualism, yet he had learned French through immersion programs while serving as staff chief with the Canadian army's mobile command in St. Hubert, Quebec. Waters insisted that he had no intention of relearning French at his age, but he did admit to listening occasionally to the French news broadcasts on Radio Canada.

He railed against the "tyranny of the minorities" that led to government grants for "black lesbians from Dartmouth" and "groups working on banana horticulture." He also preached tolerance for the racist regime in South Africa. Yet he founded the Calgary Native Opportunities Committee and advocated Native sharing of commercial wealth and prosperity.

He promoted industrial growth and roundly declared that environmental dangers were exaggerated. He recommended spending Alberta Heritage Fund money on diversion of northern waters into southern Alberta river basins. Yet he fished those waters for salmon and was an organizing member of the International Wildlife Association.

His late chance for a political career came after a distinguished career in the military and in business. Born in Winnipeg in 1920, Waters attended private high school in Calgary and at the University of Alberta in Edmonton before joining the Fourteenth Army Tank Battalion (Calgary regiment) as a private in 1940. After serving in England, he returned to Canada to be commissioned. He then volunteered for parachute training and was posted to the First Special Service Force, a unique U.S.-Canadian assault unit being secretly formed in Montana to face the enemy overseas.

The parachute unit was the first dual-nation fighting force to serve as a combat unit with the Allied armies. It became popularly known as the Devil's Brigade after Hollywood made a movie about the unit in 1968. The name "devil" referred to the fact that members blackened their faces for night raids. Waters served with the unit in the Aleutians and in Italy. He earned his U.S. Silver Star for a 1944 mission during the Italian campaign when he was serving as a major temporarily in charge of a casualty-stricken battalion. Waters walked under direct fire to coordinate his infantry unit with a supporting tanks regiment for a successful attack on an enemy-held mountain village.

After the war Waters remained in the military and became chief instructor at the Joint Air Training Centre at Rivers, Manitoba. He then held staff appointments in Ottawa. In 1953 he commanded the Second Battalion of the Princess Patricia's Canadian Light Infantry in Germany, later returning to Canada to convert them to a parachute battalion, part of the Canadian Airborne Regiment.

Waters served in a variety of liaison and military observer postings with the United States Marine Corps, the United Nations, and NATO, then became commander, Mobile Command, at St. Hubert, Quebec—in effect the army's operational commander. He retired from the armed forces in 1975 with the rank of lieutenant general. He then became a captain of industry, working for Calgary billionaire Fred C. Mannix and heading companies involved in an assortment of commercial construction projects.

Waters retired from the Mannix empire in 1989 at age sixty-nine and immediately embraced what seemed to be a futile cause. He became the western-based Reform Party's candidate in an Alberta senatorial election that offered no guarantee of a subsequent Senate appointment. The provincial government had grown tired of waiting for Prime Minister Brian Mulroney to fill an absent Senate seat and called a vote to discover whom Albertans would like to see chosen.

Although he had no previous political experience, Waters proved to be an accomplished campaigner. A skilled and humorous speaker given to lacing his words with quotations from Winston Churchill, Waters even made political hay of his age. If appointed senator, he could only serve six years before compulsory retirement at seventy-five, and that period exactly coincided with the Reform Party's timetable for Senate reform. Contrary to many expectations, Waters scored an election victory with 265,000 votes—more than twice that of his nearest rival.

Waters wasn't the preferred candidate of Alberta's Conservative premier, Don Getty, but Getty was gracious. He swallowed his Tory pride and undertook to support the Reformer. Mulroney vacillated for eight months. He finally agreed to make Waters's Senate appointment official when Getty threatened to withdraw Alberta's support for the Meech Lake constitutional accord, a national-unity initiative that subsequently foundered. Mulroney declared that Waters's appointment would be strictly a "one-shot deal."

Waters spent his time as a senator focusing more on the way he had arrived than on the job itself. He was criticized for having one of the lowest attendance records in the upper house, but he did oppose the goods and services tax and said he always participated in major votes.

He had little more than one year to enjoy what he called "the place where longevity was created." In July 1991 Waters was diagnosed with brain cancer. Three months later, at age seventy-one, he was dead. Seven years later Alberta renewed its push for Senate reform by holding an election for two so-called "senators in waiting." But this time around, the prime minister of the day, Jean Chretien, was not so willing to appoint the winners to the upper house. Eighteen months after their election, senators-in-waiting Bert Brown and Ted Morton were still waiting. The appointment of Edmonton musician Tommy Banks to the Senate in April 2000 suggested they would be waiting for a long time.

Clarence "Big" Miller

Blues singer

1923–1992

When Big Miller made Edmonton his home in 1969, he had the same goal as all the settlers who had come before him. He wanted a fresh start and the opportunity to put his skills to good use. In Alberta he hoped to revitalize his career as a blues singer. Audiences elsewhere wanted lounge singers who performed "Feelings" and "Melancholy Baby." They no longer cared about a big black bluesman who sang about being broke and hungry and feeling low-down.

Miller had done plenty of hard travelling before coming to Alberta. During the best of times, he had sung with a who's who of jazz legends: Count Basie, Duke Ellington, Miles Davis, Woody Herman, and Lionel Hampton. On his own United Artists and Savoy albums, he was marketed as a "sexy crooner." During the tough times he played smoky barrooms from his home town of Kansas City to Canberra to Honolulu and back.

The lowest low point in Miller's life came in the early 1960s, when the 350-pound singer was stuck in Vancouver without money, left stranded and penniless by a booking agent who failed to pay him after a concert tour of the Pacific Northwest. In desperation, Miller took a job at a sing-along pizza joint, leading the singing and playing trombone with a honky-tonk pianist. It wasn't the Sands in Vegas, nor was it the kind of music that Miller particularly liked to play. One can only do so many choruses of "Roll Out the Barrel" and "Bill Bailey, Won't You Please Come Home?" before regurgitating one's pizza. But at least it gave him some breathing space and a chance to see what other possibilities Canada might have to offer. Upset by the growing racial tensions in his own country, he was eager to leave the United States behind.

In 1964 Miller made his first trip to Alberta, where he found plenty of opportunities to play and sing the blues. He also found a place virtually free of the violence and prejudice he had encountered in the United States and abroad. In Edmonton he performed at such clubs as the Embers, the Saxony Motor Inn, and the Sheraton Caravan Penthouse. He also had a regular spot on CFRN Radio. In Calgary he injected a dose of the blues into the mix of hoe-down and country fiddle music featured in the city's nightspots during Stampede, and he was often featured on the marquee of a club called Fernando's Hideaway.

Between 1964 and 1974 Miller and his trio travelled widely throughout Alberta, playing bars and hotels from Lethbridge to Grande Prairie. The work was steady, but it was a hard slog, especially in the smaller centres. "They didn't dig it," he said. "They didn't understand what I was trying to do." Miller wanted to sing the blues, but rural audiences wanted to hear Charley Pride tunes.

He finally turned to Alberta Culture for help, somehow persuading the bureaucrats that the blues—the music of biker bars and strip joints—should be marketed throughout the province as a respectable educational project. He wasn't selling out, he said. For Miller, the government gig was simply a case of the hustler hustling. Before long Miller was showcasing his music in schools and community halls, backed by a sixteen-piece band. He travelled to Japan as Alberta's musical emissary and was featured in *Big and the Blues,* a National Film Board documentary.

In 1985, when Athabasca University gave him an honorary doctorate in humanities, Miller was overwhelmed almost to tears. "You all too much, man, you all too much," he told the convocation audience. Later he joked about the award. "Now you can call me Doctor Big," he quipped. Nobody ever called him by his first name, Clarence.

In 1991 Miller joined forces with Calgary modern dance company Decidedly Jazz Danceworks to create a show commemorating his life and times. He was to sing and talk about his life while the company danced to the music of a five-piece band.

Miller hadn't talked much about his life since coming to Alberta. Like many newcomers, he preferred to leave the past behind, so he never did reveal, for example, how he managed to work in New York during the 1950s, when the Mafia controlled all the clubs, or what happened to his short-lived marriage.

But he did talk about racism, the ugly side of human nature that he had encountered while growing up in Kansas City during the 1930s as the gospel-singing son of a Sioux Indian minister and a black mother. He encountered racism while serving in the American army during the Second World War and while travelling through the United States as a musician. White musicians were allowed to eat in restaurants and drink with the customers. Miller ate in the kitchen and drank in his hotel room.

In Alberta, while he could see himself as a "fly in the buttermilk," he felt safe from racial prejudice. Now and again, however, racism reared its ugly skinhead. He recalled his shock at an incident that had occurred one night while he was driving home from a gig along Whyte Avenue in Edmonton. He had stopped to let four young men cross the street and they responded by rocking his car and taunting him with racial slurs.

For Miller, it was a disturbing reminder of what he believed he had left behind. He had thought of Alberta as a refuge from discrimination, a place where a black high school dropout could receive a university degree and teach a master class in jazz and blues to the white kids at the prestigious Banff Centre. Now, perhaps, it was something uglier than that.

He never performed the show with Decidedly Jazz Danceworks. During rehearsals Miller was taken to hospital with a bleeding ulcer, and the show was postponed for a year. In June 1992, during rehearsals for the rescheduled show, Miller suffered a heart attack and died, at age sixty-nine. But the show went on. It became a memorial tribute to the black bluesman from the American Midwest who had found a welcome in the white-jazz capitals of western Canada.

The dancers said they hoped to take the show, entitled *No Small Feets,* to some of the towns where Miller had played during his long life on the road. The Miller legacy has also been preserved in a compilation album put together in 1997 by Edmonton's perennial man about music and later Canadian senator, Tommy Banks. Banks culled the recordings of Miller's late-1970s sessions with CBC Radio. Aside from one live album released in the 1980s, there hadn't been a proper Big Miller release since the 1950s, Banks said. "And they're all out of print in any case."

Toward the end of his life, Big Miller took to billing himself as the Last of the Blues Shouters. He had come a long way from Kansas City. The hustler had never stopped hustling and the audience, in Alberta at least, had never tired of listening.

Roloff Beny

Photographer

1924 –1984

Roloff Beny called himself the Marco Polo of Medicine Hat. Although he lived in Rome and pronounced the name of his home town, Italian style, "Meddi-chee-nee Hat," he always seemed to take some perverse pleasure in telling people he was from a part of the world that most of his high-society friends had never heard of.

He was born Wilfrid Roy Beny in Medicine Hat in 1924, the son of a patriotic, Liberal-voting General Motors dealer who named him after Sir Wilfrid Laurier and hoped that one day he would take over the dealership.

But Beny had no intention of making a career out of selling cars and trucks. At age seven, he told his parents he was going to be a painter. He took lessons from a local teacher, won a scholarship to the Banff School of Fine Arts at age fifteen, then moved to Toronto and eventually New York to pursue further training.

His penchant for collecting famous friends surfaced early. University of Toronto roommate Lesley Blanch recalled that Beny could enter a room full of strangers and immediately know the right people to socialize with. "He was drawn to power, wealth, and beauty."

Beny was living in a cold-water apartment on New York's East Side in 1947 when he received his big break. The Brooklyn Museum awarded him a prize for a suite of his colour engravings, collectively titled *Ecclesiastes*. An art agent who saw the show sold his engravings for $1,000. The next day, Beny moved into a Madison Avenue pent-house. He was twenty-three.

Two years later Beny held his first one-man retrospective in Toronto. During a trip home to Lethbridge, where his parents had reestablished after leaving Medicine Hat, Beny told a reporter that his upbringing had influenced his painting. "I feel my work would not be complete if I had not been brought up on the Prairies," he said. "It has given a depth and a perspective to my work which wouldn't be there if I had grown up in mid-Manhattan."

Beny would not always speak so fondly of his birthplace. During a subsequent visit to Lethbridge, he was required to surrender his pet Lhasa terrier to customs and immigration authorities for quarantining. The dog died while in detention. "Of a broken heart," said Beny. He vowed never to set foot in Alberta again.

In 1956, after a successful photographic exhibition in London, Beny permanently traded his paintbrushes for camera lenses. He moved to Rome and adopted the first name Roloff—his mother's maiden name—because he thought the name Wilfrid was not chic enough for a self-styled *artiste* who wanted to set the international art world on fire. His friends, however, would always refer to him affectionately as "Wilfie."

Beny always bristled at the suggestion that he was a "mere" photographer, insisting that he was as much an artist as a painter or sculptor. He told reporters that he "painted" with his lens, and he described his work in terms of brush strokes, canvases, and "the alchemy of light."

He achieved an international reputation for his sumptuous coffee-table books, which featured the art and architecture of the ancient and classical worlds, especially the Greco-Roman world of the Mediterranean coastal regions. Because the books were hugely expensive to produce, he relied on wealthy patrons to finance them. The Eaton family sponsored his 1967 book, *To Everything There is a Season,* commissioned for Canada's centennial.

His most controversial sponsors were the shah and empress of Iran, for whom he produced two books, *Iran: Elements of Destiny* and *Persia: Bridges of Turquoise.* In keeping with all of his picture books, they showed only the grandeur of the country and gave no hint of the misery and rot associated with life under the shah.

Beny defended his stylistic approach, saying it was beauty that stimulated him esthetically, not the ugly and the downtrodden. He surrounded himself with beautiful things and people, hosting lavish parties in his Rome penthouse that were attended by the likes of Gore Vidal, Salvador Dali, Federico Fellini, and Pierre Trudeau. "Beny needed famous people the way addicts need cocaine," journalist Robert Fulford said. Every time Beny gave a media interview, he left the reporter with a notebook full of quotes about Vivien Leigh, Laurence Olivier, Lord Snowdon, and Pablo Picasso.

Beny's artistic life was played out against an appropriate backdrop. Rome, from the late 1950s onward, was the cultural hub of postwar Europe. This was the centre of Gian Carlo Menotti's newly formed Spoleto festival, the literature and films of Pier Paulo Pasolini, and the neo-realist cinema of Fellini and Luchino Visconti.

Beny's personal life also flowered in Italy. Once he had declared himself to be homosexual, he no longer felt welcome in Canada. "I've ceased to expect much recognition there," he said in a 1978 interview. "It doesn't concern me that much. I've had as much recognition as anybody could expect in Canada, but it's not the identity and warmth I've found in Italy." His narcissism didn't help to endear him to Canadian critics. He once sent out Christmas cards featuring a naked picture of himself holding a naked picture of himself.

In 1979 he had another dust-up with the people of his native province when the Alberta government withdrew an offer to buy his entire personal collection of negatives and prints. The government cancelled the deal amid New Democratic Party opposition claims that the collection would cost taxpayers more than $545,000. From his Rome apartment, Beny announced he was "devastated and deeply disappointed."

Beny suffered another reverse that same year, when the Islamic revolution knocked the peacock throne of Iran off its pedestal and forced the shah to abdicate. Beny was left begging for the money owed to his Toronto publisher, McClelland and Stewart, for distributing the two books about Iran. The four other books about Iran on his drawing board never found a sponsor.

Disappointment shadowed the rest of Beny's life. He died in his bathtub of a brain hemorrhage in March 1984 at age sixty.

For a while it seemed as if his legacy might disappear with him. Critics dismissed his work as sentimental and old-fashioned, the product of a romantic's obsession with beauty at the expense of messy reality. The photographic collection that the Alberta government had rejected for purchase in 1979 was also rejected by the Smithsonian Institution. Eventually it was given away to the National Archives of

Canada, where it gathered dust in a storeroom for half a dozen years.

But during the 1990s Beny became fashionable again. In 1993 the Royal Ontario Museum in Toronto opened a Roloff Beny Gallery. The following year *Visual Journeys,* a book of Beny's photography, was published, and an exhibition of photos from the book was installed in the Royal Ontario Museum. The University of Lethbridge added a selection of Beny's photographs to its Canadian and Early Twentieth Century collections.

In 1996 the National Archives mounted an exhibition of his photographs entitled *Legends in Life and Art: The Portrait Photography of Roloff Beny.* The photographs, done on assignment for such magazines as *Vogue* and *Harper's Bazaar,* featured such icons of the artistic and fashion worlds as Rudolf Nureyev, Glenn Gould, Coco Chanel, and Tennessee Williams. After showing in Ottawa, the exhibition travelled to eight international capitals, including Madrid, Paris, and Vienna. "His art was a metaphor for his life as a gay man," said exhibition curator Edward Tompkins. "That's one of the reasons the collection is important. He was a gay Canadian artist who made it on the international stage when not so many did."

Bill Pratt

President of the Calgary Winter Olympics

1928–1999

Bill Pratt said he would like to be remembered as the man who built Heritage Park, a frontier village in Calgary where summer visitors cruise the Glenmore Reservoir in a working replica of a vintage sternwheeler and winter visitors go dashing through the snow in a one-horse open sleigh.

People in the news, however, rarely get to decide where posterity will place them. Nixon will always be remembered for Watergate. Salieri will be remembered for having been jealous of Mozart. And Bill Pratt will be remembered as the tough-talking guy in the white cowboy hat who coordinated the construction of ski jumps, bobsled runs, and other sports facilities for the 1988 Calgary Winter Olympics.

Pratt was not, as some newspaper reports after his death suggested, the man who actually brought the Olympics to Calgary. Credit for that goes to oilman Frank King and other members of the Calgary Booster Club, a group of businessmen who raised money for amateur sport. They formed the team that put forward the successful bid for the games in September 1981. Pratt came aboard two years later, when organizers needed a strong, experienced business manager.

King was serving as volunteer chairman of the organizing committee when Pratt joined the Olympics team, and the pair were soon characterized by the media as a Jekyll and Hyde combination.

The difference in their personal styles could not have been more marked. Tall, lean, and baby-faced, King was the smooth-talking diplomat who could charm politicians and cynical journalists. Pratt was short, barrel-chested, and aggressive—he had no time for "bullshit or wimps."

The combination worked. King said he and Pratt rarely disagreed on the bigger issues. Pratt had what King called a "gut feel" for what to do, and Pratt was invariably right.

Pratt had developed his management style while getting his hands dirty on construction sites. Born in Ottawa, he was the youngest child of a hockey-loving civil servant named Ford Pratt and his wife, Ruth, an actress and competitive distance swimmer. Bill came west at age twenty to take a summer job as truck driver on an Alberta construction project owned by his father's friend Red Dutton, a National Hockey League hockey star who became a successful real estate developer.

That summer job turned into a full-time position and provided an opportunity for Pratt to make a career in the Dutton organization. He became chief assistant and troubleshooter for Dutton, whom he described as "my second father and mentor." Pratt built roads, office buildings, dams, and railway lines, and showed little patience for shirkers and incompetents. He said he "kicked asses and cleaned up messes." Pratt was the troubleshooter with a reputation for tackling all the dirty work that nobody else wanted to do.

His commitment and devotion to duty brought certain rewards. During the 1950s Pratt oversaw construction of Calgary's first shopping centre, Chinook Plaza. He completed the project on time and under budget and received a bonus from Dutton: two new suits. But the ultimate reward eluded him. Instead of assuming control of Dutton's empire when the old man retired in the late 1960s, Pratt landed on the unemployment line. Dutton sold his holdings, and Pratt found himself out of work.

He looked for a job that would, in some manner, recapture the life-affirming experience he had undergone during the early 1960s, when he took a sabbatical from the Dutton firm to help build Heritage Park. He always remembered how Calgarians expressed their delight when they paid their first visit to what is now Canada's largest living historical village. "This is better than money," said Pratt. "It's leaving something behind for people."

In 1970 Pratt found another job in which he could leave something behind for people. He became general manager of the Calgary Exhibition and Stampede, an organization for which he had started volunteering shortly after moving to Calgary. He had been the Stampede's original courtesy car driver, and his first customer was Bing Crosby.

During his ten years as Stampede manager, Pratt consolidated his reputation as a builder who could get the job done. He expanded Stampede Park and built a new racetrack and grandstand complex. Then he became project manager for the Saddledome ice arena, located on the Stampede grounds. The arena later became both the home rink for the Calgary Flames and Calgary's first Olympic facility.

At the time of his Saddledome appointment, Pratt was not a household name in Calgary. But that changed within a couple of years when reports that the arena project was $9 million over budget began to appear in the media. Pratt was stung by the reports, which blamed him for the cost overrun, but he could do little to counteract the negative publicity. A contractual gag order prevented him from publicly defending himself.

As it turned out, the Saddledome's budget problems were typical for Calgary during that boom period of high construction costs. Virtually every other public project at the time was experiencing cost overruns that were much worse. But the sky-is-falling media reports—hyperbolized with references to the $1.1-billion deficit of the Montreal Olympics—did their damage, and Pratt found himself tainted with controversy.

Controversy dogged him for the five years that he served as president of the Olympics. Whenever staff were shuffled or fired or anything else went wrong in the organization, the blame always landed at Pratt's door. He couldn't understand why the media seemed to hate him so much. He remained bitter when the games were over. He didn't think the scars would ever heal.

After the Olympics, Pratt worked with a team of oil well firefighters in Kuwait. He then teamed up again with Frank King on the committee organizing the Calgary events for Canada 125—the celebration of the nation's 125th birthday in 1992. That same year, 1992, Pratt was named an officer of the Order of Canada.

Pratt's last big project was the Trans Canada Trail, a sixteen-thousand-kilometre recreational pathway that will span the country when completed. Pratt was the founding executive director of the Trail Foundation, which began life as a legacy project of Canada 125.

In 1997, when Pratt was stricken with Lou Gehrig's disease, he handled the diagnosis with typical stoicism. If he died, so be it, he said. Dying was just nature taking its course. He became involved in various projects to raise money for research and to heighten public awareness of the disease.

Pratt died in November 1999 at age seventy-one. Friends and colleagues noted that his bulldog style had often gotten in the way of the public recognition he might have earned for his contributions. But in time the emphasis would shift from his style to what he had actually given to his community. A long-ago headline summarized his great achievement: "Pratt's specialty is getting things built."

Alexander Gray

Opera singer and artistic director

1929–1998

Alexander Gray was a talented baritone—good enough to sing lead roles with the Canadian Opera Company for sixteen years—which means he could have made a very good living for himself by just being a performer.

But Gray was one of those generous people who want to do more than capitalize on their talents. He wanted to give something back and he did. He was the founding artistic director of what is now the Calgary Opera, and he played a key role in the early development of the Banff Centre, as head of the opera division. He also started what was to be Calgary's first fully professional company for staging big Broadway musicals.

The Broadway musical venture failed after just one production, *The Sound of Music*. But give the man full marks for trying—he was the only one to ever do so.

Gray was at the height of his musical powers when he moved to Calgary in 1971 at age forty-two. Born in Lachine, near Montreal, in 1929, he had been performing professionally since he was seventeen. He had just completed a two-year stint as principal baritone with the Kiel State Opera on West Germany's Baltic coast when he received the call to come to Calgary.

The call came from Richard Johnston, Gray's old friend and former singing teacher, who was creating a musical centre at the relatively new University of Calgary where talented musicians could compose and perform in the shadow of the Canadian Rockies. Up the road, in the Rockies themselves, the inaugural Banff Festival of the Arts was emerging as a small event with great expectations. "A rival to Salzburg?" asked the headline in a local newspaper. The hills were indeed alive with the sound of music.

Johnston's offer to Gray was a temporary, Canada Council-funded position as resident musician at the University of Calgary.

Gray said he liked the idea of coming to Calgary to work with an old friend whose energy he found contagious. For his part, Johnston felt fortunate to have a performer of Gray's calibre available to provide inspiration for his students.

Gray gave his first Calgary recital a few weeks after his arrival and local reviewers were ecstatic. "The only apt description could be spellbinding," wrote Bill Musselwhite in the *Calgary Herald.* "If any University of Calgary official lets Alexander Gray leave the university, he deserves to be certified incompetent."

Gray did not leave. His temporary position became full time, and he remained at the university for the next twenty-three years, teaching in the faculty of music. He also taught and staged musicals and operas at what is now the Banff Centre, and he maintained a full schedule of guest singing engagements with opera companies across North America and abroad, performing such roles as Dr. Malatesta in *Don Pasquela* with the Goldovsky Opera Theatre and Escamillo in *Carmen* at the Edmonton Opera.

In 1975 Gray became the founding artistic director of the Calgary Opera, then the Southern Alberta Opera Association. A group of Calgary businessmen and music lovers wanted the city to have an opera company, and Gray made it happen. It was his duty to do such pioneering things, he said. His mandate as a member of Johnston's team at the University of Calgary was to use his talent to serve the wider community.

Gray used his talent in many ways. As a singer, he said he had as much fun playing such musical comedy roles as Tevye in *Fiddler on the Roof* or Don Quixote in *Man of La Mancha* as he did essaying the roles of Figaro in *The Barber of Seville* or Marcello in *La Boheme.*

"I tell my students never to pass up an opportunity to try something different," he said as he prepared to star in *Man of La Mancha* at the Banff Centre in 1972.

His own performing, before he arrived in Calgary, had encompassed playing summer stock theatre under the big Melody Fair tent in Toronto during the 1950s and performing in Gilbert and Sullivan productions on the Stratford Festival's Avon Theatre stage during the early 1960s. He had also sung on CBC Radio and appeared in CBC Television productions of *Otello* and *Rigoletto* in the days when the national broadcaster still had its own opera company. It was a busy time, he said, and he felt lucky to have been a part of it.

During the twenty years before he settled in Calgary, Gray had also toured extensively, performing a concert program that ranged, he said, from "arcane French art songs and German lieder to operetta hits." And he had sung short-term opera engagements throughout the United States.

Because of his busy touring schedule, Gray rarely saw his family. His children, sons Dave, Brian, and Andy, later became auto mechanics rather than follow their father into music. Gray didn't mind. They were all happy, he said. What more could a father ask for?

Perhaps his greatest musical challenge came in 1986, when Gray and his wife, the former Joyce Hill—a one-time dancer with Canada's National Ballet—joined forces with two other couples to mount a week-long, fully professional production of *The Sound of Music* at Calgary's twenty-seven-hundred-seat Jubilee Auditorium. The couples pooled $200,000 for the production. Everyone would be paid, Gray said, including the children.

Gray had hoped to take the profits from that show, which received no government or corporate grants of any kind, and put them toward subsequent Calgary productions of such popular musicals as *Carousel, Showboat,* and *Brigadoon.* Unfortunately box-office receipts for *The Sound of Music* fell $20,000 below target, leaving Gray and his team without the funds to keep the project going.

Gray acknowledged that he had learned from the experience. But, ever the musical pioneer, he then announced plans to start up a musical theatre training school in Calgary. It would be a Canadian first, he said. Big musicals were growing more popular across North America and proper training had to be available.

That venture never got off the ground either. Heart problems finally curtailed Gray's musical activities. He retired from the university in 1994, at age sixty-five, and moved to Victoria, where he died in October 1998 at age sixty-nine.

Bob Hatfield

Physician and humourist

1929–1999

Dr. Bob Hatfield—a consulting general specialist in internal medicine at Calgary's Foothills Hospital—was diagnosed with leukemia at age sixty-one. The disease didn't stop him from working, or enjoying life, or indulging his love of humour. In fact, it gave new purpose to both his professional and his personal life. He became a living advertisement for his theory that laughter—as the *Reader's Digest* proclaims—is the best medicine.

The laughter theory has been around for centuries. During the Middle Ages, court clowns scared off the demons of disease by acting silly. In the thirteenth century, a surgeon named Andre de Mondeville urged families to cheer up their sick relatives by telling them jokes. "The body grows fat from joy and thin from sadness," de Mondeville declared.

Norman Cousins, an American magazine editor, author, humanitarian, and intellectual, popularized the theory in our own time. Cousins never went to medical school, but he held a distinguished teaching post at the University of California in Los Angeles because of his writings on medical science and the human healing system.

In 1964 a crippling spinal illness incapacitated Cousins. Fierce pain and a guarded prognosis by his physician forced him to turn inward. He mobilized himself with his sense of humour. "I discovered that ten minutes of solid belly laughter would give me two hours of pain-free sleep," he reported later. Sedimentation tests showed that the inflammation levels in his body dropped whenever he laughed at comedy films. He wrote about his recovery in the *New England Journal of Medicine.*

Hatfield—a Calgary-born physician who spent more than forty years working in internal medicine—was captivated by Cousins's *Journal* article.

"It was the old story of having some personal conviction, sometimes hard to enunciate, and suddenly you are hearing another person say exactly what you think," said Dr. Bob.

Nobody ever called him Dr. Hatfield. It was always Dr. Bob. His older brother Bruce was also an internal medicine specialist in Calgary, so it made sense to call them by their first names.

Dr. Bob said he was drawn to Cousins's writings about the positive impact of humour on health because the author was intelligent, wise, and persuasive. "Here was a man who made his living by being thoughtful," said Dr. Bob. "And he was saying that humour had some power."

Subsequent scientific research noted numerous beneficial effects of laughter on the human body—from lowered blood pressure to increased numbers of disease-battling immune cells.

Dr. Bob did not participate in any of the research, but he was happy to spread the word. At the time of his leukemia diagnosis in 1991, he was actively promoting the use of humour as a medical tool, stocking his waiting room with comic books instead of *Time* magazine and *Maclean's*, and looking for ways to formally establish humour as part of the healing culture at Foothills Hospital.

Dr. Bob had always included the human side of healing as a tool in his medicine box. During the 1970s newspapers reported that he was one of the only doctors in the city—aside from psychiatrists and psychologists—who set aside one afternoon a week to listen to patients discussing their illnesses, both physical and emotional. With a seventy-hour-a-week workload at Foothills Hospital, plus a busy internal medicine practice that he ran with his brother, Dr. Bob did not have much time to listen to patients talk about their problems. But he always found the time.

Also during the 1970s, Dr. Bob turned his attention to another branch of medicine that emphasized the human being rather than the disease being treated. He and Dr. Bruce became pioneers in the emerging science of palliative care—bringing pain relief and comfort to the dying.

The two brothers, once referred to in a newspaper headline as the "Real McCoys"—they did, in fact, claim distant kinship with the famous nineteenth-century Hatfields of West Virginia—closed their internal medicine practice in 1992 after serving patients for thirty-three years. But they did not retire completely. Both continued to work at Foothills Hospital, where Dr. Bob's daily routine always started with the comics page of the newspaper.

"The comics first, the deaths second, the sports section third, and then the front page," he said. "If there's any time left over, I'll read the city news. But comics first. And I just have to share."

If a patient hadn't heard of "Calvin and Hobbes," a now discontinued newspaper comic strip dealing with the mischievous adventures of a spiky-haired little boy and his imaginary tiger, Dr. Bob would be happy to bring in a clipping from the newspaper. "And if I get a flicker, I'll tell you there are whole, thick books of this little character."

The key to using humour to heal, he said, was not to force the humour on the patient but to let it evolve naturally through the bond that develops between doctor and patient.

"Part of establishing that bond is to let you know a little bit about me. And I will learn more about you than just that you've got cancer. Where's your family? What do you do for work? And being a Calgarian by birth, I know quite a number of people around town. So I can make pretty realistic links with a lot of people."

Dr. Bob preferred to keep his leukemia diagnosis to himself, and few of his patients knew he was ill. After the diagnosis, his name began to appear regularly on the religion pages of the newspaper as he dedicated himself to church work, conducting workshops on life and death issues for United Church congregations. He enjoyed woodworking and photographing wildflowers, and he always took the opportunity to deliver the message that laughter is good therapy. He died in April 1999, at age sixty-nine, at his home in Calgary.

Glen Gorbous

Baseball player

1930–1990

"Glen Gorbous isn't remembered by many people," said the 1973 edition of *Who's Who in Professional Baseball.* "Not much of a hitter, and not much speed afoot. But oh, how he could throw!"

Oh, indeed, how he could throw. That's what the *Guinness Book of World Records* people must have thought when they listed Gorbous as follows: "Longest baseball throw. Glen Gorbous (Canada) threw a baseball 445 ft., 10 in. on August 1, 1957."

Gorbous claimed another record-making achievement in addition to his throw. He was the first athlete from southern Alberta to play in a major-league baseball game. He did so in 1955, when he started playing with the Cincinnati Reds.

Another player from southern Alberta, Floyd Spackman of Stirling, cut his own slice of the American dream pie in 1955, when he struck out both Mickey Mantle and Yogi Berra in a preseason warm-up between the New York Yankees and the St. Louis Cardinals. But Spackman never made it to the big show. He injured his knee during spring training, went back to university, finished a degree in petroleum engineering, and came to Calgary to work in the oilpatch.

Spackman always thought of baseball as being no more than a hobby. For Gorbous, it was much more. As a child, he had learned that he could throw, and he wanted that arm to take him to the top.

Gorbous grew up in the coal-mining town of Rosedale, outside Drumheller. With nothing much to do during the summer months, young Glen and his pals would spend their time flinging rocks across the Red Deer River. Glen was one of the few kids who could hit the opposite bank. He did so with every throw.

The American-born owner of the Rosedale lumberyard taught Gorbous the rudiments of baseball. By his early teens, he was playing third base and relief pitcher for the Rosedale Midways, who became junior provincial champions.

When Gorbous turned sixteen, his family moved to Vulcan, where his father opened a furniture store. Gorbous commuted to Calgary to play for the semi-pro Purity 99 team in the Alberta Big Four League, and he quickly established himself as a league star. The Brooklyn Dodgers heard about him and came to Calgary to take a look. The scout said, "Gorbous, you have a fair arm." With that faint-praise endorsement, Gorbous was on his way to the show.

He began his professional career with the Dodgers playing for the club's farm team in Medford, Oregon, in a ballpark that doubled as a rodeo arena. "Lots of hoof prints, and lots of horse manure," he recalled. "In the outfield, you'd back up and catch a fly ball in Chute Number Four."

He left Medford after two years and went back to playing semi-professional ball for the Purity 99 team in Calgary. One year later he was back in the Dodgers farm system, now headed for the major leagues. Legendary Dodgers manager Tommy Lasorda, whose own major-league pitching career had been a bust, called Gorbous "the all-Canadian boy with the all-American arm."

As it turned out, Gorbous never actually played a game for the Dodgers. He started with the Cincinnati Reds in 1955 and one year later moved to the Philadelphia Phillies. After a year there, he was traded to the St. Louis Cardinals because of his inconsistent hitting. He had a major-league batting average of .238. The Cards sent him to their Triple A team in Omaha, Nebraska. That's where the all-Canadian boy, as a $200 promotional stunt, threw the ball that gave him his place in the history of the all-American sport.

To visualize his throwing feat, think of a baseball travelling one and one-half times the length of a Canadian football field. That's what Gorbous achieved on a muggy evening in August 1954. "Oh, my arm hurt after," he said. "Next morning, I couldn't even comb my hair."

Gorbous remained in the minor leagues for a few years until he lost his enthusiasm for the game. In 1959, at age twenty-nine, he called it quits and moved back to Vulcan to take over his father's furniture store.

In 1978 Gorbous relocated to Calgary. He went on the road as a salesman for an Edmonton company that provided housing and catering for oilpatch exploration camps in the northern wilderness. From time to time, sports reporters would rediscover him and write about his long throw. Gorbous was flattered by the attention, but he noted sadly that his moment in the sun had passed. "When I go up to a place like Tuktoyaktuk, they're not too impressed with me up there."

Gorbous died in June 1990 at his Calgary home while recovering from open-heart surgery. He was fifty-nine. Would anyone ever surpass his throwing achievement? After more than forty years, the record remains intact.

Johnny Bright

Football player and school administrator

1931–1983

Johnny Bright was a black man who fought against great odds to stand tall among the giants in a white man's game.

College football today is a fully integrated sport. Blacks and whites play together on the same squads, and they play against other teams with both black and white players. This was unheard of in 1951. Bright learned this the hard way the day he played quarterback for Drake University against Oklahoma State, and a white opponent deliberately smashed his jaw. "Prejudice was a way of life for many," he said afterwards. "I was the first black to play against Oklahoma."

A white player fractured Bright's jaw with an elbow smash after Bright threw a touchdown pass. The attack was aimed at putting him out of the game, and when Bright refused to leave, the same player came back to crack his jaw a second time. Bright ended up making a painful, all-night ride to Des Moines, Iowa, for treatment because no hospital in Oklahoma would treat a black.

A *Life* magazine photographer was on hand to capture the entire seven-minute incident on film. The resulting double-page spread gave the photographer a Pulitzer Prize and made Bright an international celebrity.

"That was the greatest learning factor of my life," Bright said. "That seven minutes did more to teach me the simple basic rights and wrongs, respect for my fellow man, and the fact that, out there, there is always somebody who—when the chance comes—will do you in."

In 1952, one year after the incident in Oklahoma, Bright turned down an offer to play for the National Football League's Philadelphia Eagles and came to Canada instead to discuss joining Les Lear's Calgary Stampeders. The January temperature was forty below when he arrived, and the Calgary airport looked to him like a "shack in the middle of nowhere." He had just one question for the Stampeder team officials: "When is the next plane out of here?" He decided to stay, however, when they told him he would earn $12,500 for the season. "Up to that time, I'd hardly ever seen anything bigger than a five-dollar bill."

Bright was an all-star forward and a leading rusher with the Stampeders, but after a shoulder injury and an appendix operation, he was labelled injury prone. After three games of the 1953 season, he was sent to Edmonton "on loan."

Calgary's loss became the Eskimos's ace in the hole. Bright helped lead Edmonton to three consecutive Grey Cup victories, in 1954, '55, and '56. His teammates dubbed him "Ole Eyebrows" because of his bushy eyebrows. He won rushing titles and received all-star honours. In 1959 he became the first black to win the Schenley Award as most valuable player in the Canadian Football League.

In 1964, at age thirty-three, Bright retired from football and became a teacher. He had earned his bachelor of education at the University of Alberta during the off season. He taught at Edmonton's Old Scona High School, Bonnie Doon, and Stratford Junior High. When he was named principal of Hillcrest Junior High in 1970, Bright became the first black school administrator in western Canada. He served as principal there until 1981, when he moved to D.S. MacKenzie. "Youngsters are our hope for the future and [they] make me proud to be an educator," he said.

He died suddenly in December 1983 of a massive heart attack while undergoing minor knee surgery at Edmonton's University Hospital. He was just fifty-three. An autopsy revealed his heart was enlarged to twice normal size, raising questions about the risk involved in giving him a general anesthetic. A coroner said the death could not have been prevented.

The *Edmonton Journal* established a John Bright Memorial Award, which is presented annually to high school students excelling both academically and athletically. In August 1999 the Johnny Bright Sports Park was unveiled at 92nd Avenue and 163rd Street in recognition of Bright's contributions to Edmonton as an athlete, educator, and citizen. "He wasn't merely one of the greatest football players ever seen in Canada," wrote sports columnist Jim Coleman. "He was a gentleman."

"Badger" Bob Johnson

Hockey coach

1931–1991

"Badger" Bob Johnson may not have been the most successful coach in Calgary Flames history. That honour goes to Terry Crisp, the curly-haired shouter who propelled the hockey team to its first and only Stanley Cup in 1989. But Johnson, who coached the team from 1982 to 1987, was undoubtedly the most popular man ever to pace behind the Flames's bench.

He was popular with everyone—the players, the fans, and the hockey writers. The players liked him because he had as much time for the unspectacular players as he had for the stars. The fans liked him because he generated an obvious passion for the game. When he furiously rubbed his big nose, wrote feverishly in his omnipresent notebook, and wiped the imaginary sweat from his brow, you just knew that he cared. Besides, he managed to turn the Flames from a team of sluggards into a winning combination.

Sportswriters liked him because of his never-say-die optimism—he never stopped climbing the mountain that he spoke about metaphorically—and the fact that he was always good for a memorable quote.

Perhaps the most memorable was "It's a great day for hockey," a quote that still appears on hockey websites all over the Internet. Every day was a great day for hockey, according to the Badger, even the days when nothing went right.

Years after his death, hockey writers were still reminiscing in their columns about Johnson's reaction to stories they wrote in January 1986, when the Flames went for eleven games without a win. Johnson confronted reporters in the Hartford dressing room after the eleventh loss and berated them for continuing to write about "our so-called slump." For anyone else, it was a slump. For Johnson, it was a temporary setback, "nothing more than a dip."

He could even find something positive to say about a 9–1 loss to the Hartford Whalers, then the worst team in the National Hockey League. "Well, boys, that's our streak breaker," he announced cheerfully to the players. "What do you mean, 'streak breaker'?" they wailed. "We just got shellacked by the worst team in the league." True enough, Johnson agreed. "But look who scored our only goal: Jim Peplinski. And he hasn't scored in at least a month."

Sure enough, two nights later, Peplinski returned to break the streak with the winning overtime goal in a game against the Vancouver Canucks. The Flames never looked back. The 1985–86 season became their best ever to that point. They upset the previously unbeatable Edmonton Oilers in the playoffs and advanced to the Stanley Cup finals against the mighty Montreal Canadiens.

Johnson had never coached in the NHL before coming to Calgary in the summer of 1982. Born in Minneapolis in 1931, he had coached hockey and baseball at high schools and colleges and had spent fifteen seasons as hockey coach with the University of Wisconsin Badgers. That's where he got his nickname. In truth, he didn't really look like a badger. With his long nose, he looked more like an anteater.

Johnson guided the Badgers to three national titles, which led to other opportunities. He coached the American national hockey team from 1973 to 1975 and was responsible for Team USA at the Innsbruck Winter Olympics in 1976. Five years later he coached Team USA in the Canada Cup tournament. By then, reporters were calling him the best coach in hockey not working in the NHL.

General managers were starting to say the same thing. In 1982 Flames general manager and president Cliff Fletcher invited Johnson to Calgary to take over from Al MacNeil as coach of the team.

The arrangement was not a comfortable one at first. The players questioned his methods, and Johnson had doubts about his ability to coach in the NHL. Before, he had been a winner; now nothing seemed to click. Was he out of his depth?

Halfway through that first season, things began to change. The players responded differently and the Flames started winning. The first American to coach a Canadian NHL team had left his amateur days behind and was starting to make his way in the professional ranks.

The Flames made the Stanley Cup quarterfinals in each of Johnson's first two seasons, and they made history in 1986 by winning their first Campbell Conference title and their first berth in the Stanley Cup finals. Then came disappointment. The team only reached the preliminary round of the 1987 playoffs. It was time for Johnson to move on.

Two years after he left, the Flames finally won the Stanley Cup. Coach Terry Crisp had taken them to the top of the mountain that Johnson had never conquered. But the players did not forget who had started them on the journey. "We did it standing on the foundation Badger had built," said Lanny McDonald. Johnson had taught them to believe in themselves.

In 1991 Johnson finally reached the top of the mountain himself, leading the Pittsburgh Penguins to their first-ever Stanley Cup championship. The victory was particularly sweet for Johnson because the Penguins clinched the win against the North Stars in his home state of Minnesota.

The victory celebrations continued through the summer. Johnson took out his notebook and started planning for the team's defence of the title. Then tragedy struck. Johnson went to the dentist at the end of August, complaining of a toothache. When the dentist found nothing, he went to the team doctor, who diagnosed brain cancer. His famous notebook became his emergency cord during the last months of his life, when the growing tumour impeded his ability to speak.

Johnson died on 26 November 1991, at age sixty. Hockey writers paid tribute to him with unrestrained affection in their columns. Somewhere in that great hockey rink in the sky, Johnson had to be writing in his notebook, rubbing his nose, still revealing his great passion for the game he pronounced "hackey."

There were few stories of his life outside hockey. Johnson had lived for the game since he was thirteen, when he won a Minneapolis city championship as a first-year coach. The off-ice profile was that of a moderate man who didn't smoke, jogged, swam, and paid little heed to material possessions. A reporter had asked him, when he first arrived in Calgary, what kind of car he drove. Johnson couldn't remember. "I think it's a Mercury."

Why was he always so upbeat? One story offered a clue. It had to do with his daughter Diane, born with cerebral palsy and institutionalized from age seven onward at a Wisconsin state home for the mentally disabled. People who thought they had problems should pay a visit to a state home, said Johnson. They might learn to appreciate what they took for granted.

"It's a great day for hockey." That was Johnson's credo, his guiding philosophy, and his life. Words for the rest of us to live by.

Walter Twinn

Band chief, boxing promoter, and senator

1934–1997

It wasn't always easy to find Walter Twinn in Ottawa, where during his seven years as a senator he racked up one of the worst attendance records of anyone in the upper chamber. Nor was it always easy to find him in his native Slave Lake, where he used oil royalties to build a business empire of hotels, a shopping mall, truck stop, and lakeside campground. But you could invariably count on finding him in a boxing gym somewhere. In the boxing community, Twinn was always among friends. He never had to worry about criticism.

Criticism, often without qualification, seemed to follow him through all his other endeavours in business and politics. When he was appointed to the Senate in 1990, the head of the Assembly of First Nations, Georges Erasmus, dismissed Twinn as "one more wealthy individual in the Senate, like the other wealthy individuals who are already there." Nowhere in the newspaper stories about his private plane, his Cadillac limousine, and his "flamboyant lifestyle" was Twinn ever given credit for breaking free of a stultifying reserve upbringing that included residential school and poverty. As for the stories about his poor Senate attendance, none ever mentioned that his absences occurred after he suffered a heart attack in 1994.

The stories about his boxing activities, by contrast, were invariably positive. "In the boxing gyms in this town," wrote Edmonton sportswriter Robin Brownlee, "Twinn will be remembered as the man who quietly made the game go. With his money. With his passion. With a soft spot for hard-nosed kids."

Twinn's passion for boxing stemmed from his own background as a "hard-nosed kid." Born on the Sawridge Cree reserve, 250 kilometres northeast of Edmonton, he showed real promise in the ring as a boy. Later he used his boxing skills to augment his income from logging and trapping when he and his family were struggling to keep one step ahead of starvation.

Twinn finally put concerns about starvation behind him when oil was discovered on Sawridge land in 1964. Two years later he succeeded his father as chief of the small, fifty-member band and became the brains behind a series of successful business enterprises.

The band built a thirty-room hotel near the entrance to Slave Lake that later grew to 187 rooms, with a tavern and banquet hall. It also built a shopping mall, apartment complex, twenty-four-hour truck stop, and lakeside campground, and expanded Slave Lake's golf course from nine to eighteen holes. With six hundred employees, the Sawridge band became Slave Lake's biggest employer, and Twinn paid the town's largest tax bill.

Along with the investments in Slave Lake, under Twinn's leadership the Sawridge band bought sixty percent of a firm in Calgary that provided engineering services for the oil industry. They built a hotel in Jasper, bought a hotel in Fort McMurray, and took over a failed bottled water business in Vancouver, which Twinn renamed Spirit Water and predicted would outsell Evian.

Their knockouts in the corporate ring boosted the confidence of Twinn and his band colleagues and left them happily without the need for government handouts. Yet they seemed to draw nothing but public criticism for becoming big players in the world of business. When Prime Minister Brian Mulroney appointed Twinn to the Senate, critics in the Native community noted that his band had donated tens of thousands of dollars to the federal Tory party. "It's a clever move to appoint one of their people from among our people," said one aboriginal leader. "It is of no importance to the Native community."

Opposition leader Preston Manning, who had acted as an adviser to Twinn when the band first started investing Sawridge oil royalties, said the criticism was entirely predictable. "Those who make it commercially are always accused of having abandoned their heritage," Manning told an Edmonton newspaper. "They're entitled to their opinions, but Walter has been one of the few who has been successful in business. He did that by adjusting to the commercial and marketplace realities."

Besides the criticism, Twinn had another problem: A 1985 amendment to the Indian Act restored Indian status to thousands of women who had married non-Natives and paved the way for numerous claimants to seek membership in the Sawridge band. Twinn spent an estimated $2 million mounting a twelve-year legal challenge that was still continuing at the time of his death.

Twinn died of a heart attack at age sixty-three in late October 1997, after emerging from a sweat lodge at his home in Slave Lake. Native leaders praised him for "his persistence and perseverance in developing a better standard of living for Indian people." Alberta Premier Ralph Klein hailed him as "an exemplary leader, an outstanding business person, and a good friend of our province."

But the warmest words of all came from the guys down at the boxing gym who remembered Twinn fondly as their favourite, most generous, most kind-hearted uncle. "Boxing's a big part of my life, a big piece of my heart, so when we lose somebody like Walter, it's family," said one boxer. "Walter was always there," said another. "There are not a lot of people you can say that about."

Two weeks after his death, Twinn was due to attend a fight card in Prince George that he had helped put together. Instead, his ringside seat sat empty as the ring bell tolled ten times in his memory. "He was a good man," said former light-heavyweight champion Eddie "Mustafa" Muhammad about the man they called "the spit-bucket senator." "He put an awful lot into this game."

Helen Collinson
Art curator and historian
1934–1998

Helen Collinson was the daughter of a famous artist—the English-born landscape painter Henry George Glyde—and that was probably reason enough to seek a living for a while in a field other than art. She did not want to compete.

But eventually Collinson did what she was undoubtedly born to do—she followed in her father's footsteps and pursued a career in the art world. Along the way she established an international reputation for herself as the director and curator of the University of Alberta's Ring House Gallery. She also ensured her father's place in the history of art by organizing a major retrospective of his work at a time when he was no longer as prominent as he had once been.

Born in England, Collinson was a one-year-old baby in 1935 when her twenty-nine-year-old father decided to move to Calgary to teach at what is now the Alberta College of Art and Design. That seems like a remarkable journey now, given that it took place in the middle of the depression, not a time when the sons and daughters of the poor and the needy would be thinking of going to art school.

Yet, surprisingly, many did. Even at a time when society was extremely short of money, people still believed in the importance of artists, poets, and dreamers defining a cultural life for their community. Just as high school drama pioneer Betty Mitchell discovered that the poor children of Calgary loved to appear in plays dressed up as elegant ladies and gentlemen, Henry Glyde found that many of his poorer students responded to his teaching that art should be central in one's life, never a frill.

Glyde only intended to stay in Calgary for one year, but soon he was permanently hooked on the romance of the Canadian West. As his daughter later wrote, "Canada trapped him and caught his heart entirely."

Collinson spent her elementary school years in Calgary while her father taught at what was then known as the "Tech" and organized community art classes in Lethbridge and at the Medicine Hat town hall, where, he recalled, "we were admonished not to get paint on the chairs."

In 1946 the family moved to Edmonton, where Glyde established the University of Alberta's art faculty. This did not please people at the Tech, who figured that one art school in the province was enough. But Glyde wanted to spread his wings.

Collinson went to high school and university in Edmonton while her father built the University of Alberta program into a nationally respected art school. She then moved to Toronto and completed a degree in social work. During the late 1950s, she married Don Collinson and raised two daughters.

Helen Collinson worked for a number of years as a social worker with the city of Edmonton before deciding in 1970 that her father's work should, in some manner, be her work too. The university's growing collections of artworks and anthropological and zoological specimens were badly in need of organizing and cataloging. Record keeping was erratic and storage conditions substandard. Collinson joined her father as assistant curator of art exhibits and spent ten years organizing the university's objects of historical, artistic, and scientific value into a cohesive museum collection that was suitable for teaching and research purposes. The collection, which contains 17 million objects, is now considered the largest in Canada.

While she became an expert on museum objects of all kinds, it was as a curator of artworks that Collinson excelled. As director and curator of the university's Ring House Gallery, located in a campus building that was once the university president's home, she created an important showcase for Canadian artists. During her nine years with the gallery, from 1977 to 1986, she brought an international flavour and quality to the work and was the prime supporter of local Edmonton artists.

Her work was widely recognized. A former colleague says the gallery "shook the trees" by featuring work that might not otherwise have been seen in Edmonton.

Some of the more notable exhibitions presented at the gallery during Collinson's tenure were *Oh, Osiris Live Forever*—an all-encom-

passing show about mummification that brought together art, artifacts, and science—and *Now That We Are Persons,* a travelling exhibit
commemorating the fiftieth anniversary of the landmark court case
that legally recognized Canadian women as "persons" and thus entitled them to such privileges as Senate appointments.

The Ring House Gallery closed in 1986 to make way for a new
University of Alberta museum that never materialized. Collinson
devoted the next year to organizing a retrospective exhibition of her
father's drawings and paintings. Glyde had always drawn and painted
during his years at the university, endowing the Edmonton community with his murals and his costume and set designs for local theatrical productions. He had retired to Victoria in 1966 and was
almost a forgotten figure in 1987, when Collinson and Calgary curator Patricia Ainslie coordinated a show of his work at the Glenbow
Museum that brought him back into prominence. *Calgary Herald* art
critic Nancy Tousley hailed Glyde as an important regional artist who
"broke new ground in the West by using symbolic figures as a means
of exploring the Canadian spirit."

Collinson offered a more personal glimpse of her father in her
essay for the exhibition catalogue. His first sight of the Rocky
Mountains, she said, had left him "too amazed even to try to sketch."
He decided to stay in Canada, she added, because "he hadn't seen
enough of the mountains."

Collinson spent the years from 1987 to 1998 sharing her knowledge and love of art. She lent her curating expertise to such galleries
as the Whyte Museum of the Canadian Rockies in Banff, the
Medicine Hat Art Gallery, and the Red Deer Museum. She also
served overseas as a volunteer consultant in Papua, New Guinea,
Japan, and Montserrat, and sat on the board of Heritage
Interpretation International, a group dedicated to preserving the
world's cultural and natural history. In Edmonton she raised money
for local film, theatre, and history groups, and served as president of
the Edmonton Arts Council. "She did more in a week than many of
us could in a month," said a friend.

Collinson was stricken with cancer just as she was beginning to
find happiness with a new companion, Allan Sheppard. He said she
believed that two people could find joy in a new relationship even

when they knew that one of them might die soon.

Collinson died in January 1998 at age sixty-three. Her father died two months later at age ninety-one.

Grant Notley

Political leader

1939–1984

The provincial New Democrats were in terrible shape in 1968, when Grant Notley, a twenty-nine-year-old farmer's son from Didsbury, assumed the leadership of the party. As his biographer, Howard Leeson, has written, "It was a party riven with internal splits, ripe for discord, and probably about to become politically irrelevant."

So why would Notley bother? Because for him, there was no political alternative. The fact that the New Democratic Party had never held a seat in the legislature mattered little. Notley was drawn to the party for reasons that had nothing to do with its ability to win votes. A self-styled "middle-of-the-road socialist," he was interested in the social democracy movement that had started with the United Farmers of Alberta in the 1920s because it represented "the most civilized approach to blending the two instincts that we all have—our desire to be individuals and our need to be part of the community."

Notley became active in socialist politics during the late 1950s, while studying history at the University of Alberta. In 1961, when he was twenty-two, he travelled to Ottawa for the founding convention that united the Co-operative Commonwealth Federation and affiliated unions of the Canadian Labour Congress into the federal New Democratic Party. Notley stayed on for a year as national secretary then returned to Alberta to help organize the provincial New Democrats. He worked as paid provincial secretary for six years before becoming party leader.

Notley sought election three times before establishing a beachhead for the party in the provincial legislature. He ran in a rural riding, which surprised some people because it would have been more logical for him to seek office in an urban centre with a significant working-class vote. But Notley thought that media coverage and commentary would be easier to manage in a rural area, and so he chose to run in the Peace River region.

He was finally elected in 1971, the year Peter Lougheed's Tories swept most of the province with an upset victory over the ruling Social Credit party. Notley won the new riding of Spirit River-Fairview and held it for the rest of his life. He was a one-man caucus for eleven years until a second New Democrat, Ray Martin, joined him in the legislature. At that point Notley became leader of the Opposition.

In Edmonton he earned respect from his Tory colleagues for his parliamentary skills and his ability to ask intelligent questions about energy policy and health care regulations. When the government reduced oil shipments to central Canada to protest the National Energy Program—a controversial interventionist policy aimed at increasing Canadian ownership of the oil industry—Notley was the only Alberta legislator to oppose the move.

But his debating prowess and his knowledge of the bigger issues were not the only reasons that Notley earned the continuing support of his northern Alberta constituents. He also knew about the specific concerns of the rural population and respected the fact that northern members of the legislative assembly were expected to buy their clothes and their cars in the places where they sought their votes. Notley could never become a tourist in his own constituency. He had to stay in touch.

Another aspect of Notley's appeal was that while he had a well-developed social conscience and believed in the principles of social democracy, he did not come across as a traditional socialist. He had an uneasy relationship with segments of the trade union movement, and he often seemed to be grappling with the vagaries of an uncertain political life as he struggled to lead a party in the electoral wilderness. "He was not a rigid ideologue," wrote biographer Leeson. "His electoral goals dictated a flexible and even pragmatic approach to questions of public affairs."

Although he worked in Edmonton, Notley never moved to the capital city. He lived near Fairview, 559 kilometres northwest of Edmonton, in a white Cape Cod-style house on the banks of the Peace River, and commuted back and forth by air.

Notley liked air travel, which was just as well, his friends said, because he flew several times a week—and often several times a day—mostly in small planes. It was a risky way to get around, but one that northern travellers accept as a routine part of everyday life.

A plane crash ended Notley's life at age forty-five. He was returning home for the weekend on a snowy and overcast night in October 1984 when his twin-engine aircraft crashed into trees while trying to land at High Prairie. Notley had planned to take a scheduled Canadian Pacific Air flight, but when the jet was delayed by mechanical trouble, he opted to fly instead in a small Wapiti Aviation plane. A federal appeal court later ruled that Transport Canada had been negligent in enforcing safety regulations.

Political columnist Charles Lynch suggested that Notley's death would have little impact on the flying habits of people living in the northern hinterland: "What will be remembered in the end is that the man died in the crash of that Piper Navajo Chieftain—the kind of plane that northern travellers will keep climbing aboard, in fair weather or foul, because there's no other way to get around."

New Democrat hopes in conservative Alberta did not die with Notley. Although he had stood for years in the legislature as the only elected voice for his party, he clearly represented something far larger. Leeson concluded that Notley's status as a loner in opposition allowed him to speak forcefully for those who had no voice:

"In an ironic way, he succeeded because he was never too successful. In his solitary position, he could afford to speak out for the powerless, for the mistreated, for the disadvantaged."

Two years after Notley's death, the voters of Alberta sent sixteen New Democrats to the provincial legislature. It was as if Notley had made them realize that there could be a viable alternative to the dominant Tories.

"People said Grant Notley could have been a cabinet minister or premier if he was in any other party," said his legislature colleague and successor, Ray Martin. "But he cared. That was why he was in the NDP."

Sheldon Chumir

Lawyer, civil liberties advocate, and politician

1940–1992

When people spoke of Sheldon Chumir the Liberal politician, they used words like ethical, humane, scholarly, honest, and compassionate. Chumir actually managed to get himself elected on those qualities. He was one of those rare politicians who transcended party politics. Like the late New Democrat leader Grant Notley, Chumir had the personal qualities that made people forget which political party he represented.

He first became politically active in the mid-1970s, though not initially in a high-profile way. A shy loner, Chumir hated having his picture taken and would not divulge his age to reporters. He was content to remain semi-anonymous as the Calgary lawyer who said city officials should not have the power to ban political rallies in parks. Deeply committed to civil liberties, Chumir was also active in the community on issues having to do with public education, freedom of information, and police accountability.

By 1983 he could remain nameless no longer. He founded a grassroots organization called Save Public Education that put him front and centre in a high-profile campaign to stop the Calgary public school board from funding religion-based private schools.

For the first time, the veil was lifted. In a *Calgary Herald* profile, he was described as a "Jewish bachelor," former Rhodes scholar, and tax lawyer. The public did not yet know about his love of rock concerts, his collection of Kinky Friedman records, or his impish penchant for practical jokes. But the searchlight had reached into the corners and revealed that he was a Calgary grocer's son who had attended law school at the University of Alberta, played with the Golden Bears hockey and football teams, played prime minister in the university's mock parliament, reported for the *Gateway* newspaper, and been a 1963 Rhodes scholar.

Chumir worked for the federal tax department in Toronto after graduating from law school. In 1971 he became a partner and tax specialist with the Calgary law firm now known as Bennett Jones. Four years later he was running one of the biggest tax practices in the country.

Chumir left Bennett Jones in 1976 to open his own office, which specialized in civil liberties cases. "I feel people should do things that are needed in the community," he said, "not those that are popular and prestigious." He never charged for his civil liberties work. He covered his expenses with returns from his profitable investments in oil well drilling.

During the late 1970s and early 1980s, Chumir's name often appeared in the news, though not yet in the headlines. That was the way he liked it. Issues were important, he said, not personalities.

After the successful Save Public Education campaign, Chumir could no longer hide his personality. His next logical step was to run for politics, and in late 1985 he announced he would run as a Liberal candidate in the provincial riding of Calgary Buffalo. At the time, Chumir said, "the Boston Strangler was more welcome at people's doors than a Liberal." Abandoning his publicity-shy pose, he had his name printed in big letters on his campaign literature.

The "vote for the person" strategy worked. In May 1986 Chumir broke the Tory blockade of southern Alberta and became the first provincial Liberal elected in Calgary in twenty years.

By the time he ran for re-election three years later, Chumir was better known in Calgary than many Tory members of the legislative assembly. A *Calgary Herald* editorial characterized him as a "specialist in obtuse causes." But still he garnered more headlines than his Tory opponents did.

His strategy for the 1989 election was to "bribe" the voters with fridge magnets. It was a gimmicky tactic, but it worked. Chumir doubled his 1986 victory margin, thus becoming—at least by vote count—the most popular provincial politician in Calgary.

His personal popularity might have carried him to the leadership of the party, but Chumir opted to let someone else seek that job. He limited his political leadership experience to the prime ministerial role he had played in the mock parliament at university. He dropped out of the race that brought Edmonton mayor Laurence Decore to power, saying he "didn't have the fire in the belly for the position."

With Decore ensconced as party leader, Chumir played Liberal critic for all the important government portfolios, shadowing the provincial treasurer, energy minister, attorney general, and solicitor general. He also served as unpaid ombudsman for his Calgary constituents, using his legislator's salary to pay for the extra office help required. Six months after his death, people were still calling his office for help on workers' compensation claims, landlord-tenant disputes, and other matters.

Chumir died of lymphoma in 1992 at age fifty-one, three years into his second term as a member of the legislative assembly. He left the bulk of his estate for the creation of a foundation to promote ethical leadership in government, business, and community affairs. The foundation would be based on his belief—exemplified by the way he conducted his own life—that significant change for the betterment of society could only be achieved through leaders who were motivated by high ethical purpose. "There is an absence of participation by individuals in advancing the public good through public life," said Chumir. "I perceive a failure of members of our society to respond on an individual basis to a higher calling which should be part of an examined life."

On his gravestone in the Calgary Jewish cemetery, Chumir is remembered with three words: Scholar, humanitarian, legislator. A friend suggested one more: friend. "What could have been a better word for someone who always supported, gave, and helped out of his own free will?"

David Walsh

Stock promoter

1945–1998

To some people, David Walsh of Bre-X was a true local hero for a
while, a little guy who struck it big with a gold find in the Borneo
jungle reputed to be the largest the world had ever seen. To others,
after Bre-X crashed and burned, Walsh was a villain, a huckster who
led them down the yellow brick road to a pot of dirt at the end of the
rainbow. But at the end of the day, even some of his victims said
Walsh should be more pitied than scorned. Like them, he had gambled and lost.

Gambling was in Walsh's blood. His grandfather gambled on the
stock market as a broker, and so did his father. Born in August 1945,
David grew up in Montreal's Westmount district, a rich anglophone
neighbourhood. But the Walshes were too Irish, too boisterous, and
too fond of booze to really fit in.

Walsh did badly in school, and after failing a couple of grades, he
dropped out. At age nineteen he joined Montreal's Eastern Trust. He
worked the investment desk by day and took finance and accounting
classes at night. By age twenty-four he had become head of the company's investment department.

In 1976 Walsh joined Midland Doherty in Montreal as vice president of institutional equity sales. He married one of the Midland
secretaries, a multilingual cosmopolite of Armenian descent named
Jeannette Toukhmanian, and they raised two sons, Brett and Sean.
The early years of their marriage were difficult. Jeannette even went
so far as to initiate divorce proceedings, which she later dropped.

For a while it seemed as if Walsh might build a prosperous life for
himself in Montreal. His annual commissions ran into six figures
some years. But the Quebec economy was in decline, and so was
Walsh's anglophone client base.

In 1982 he decided to make a fresh start in western Canada. He
moved to Calgary, where he established an institutional equity sales

department at the Midland office there. But the oil boom was wan-
ing, and Walsh soon fell out of favour with his Calgary bosses. He
left Midland Doherty within the year and sued the company for
$110,000, claiming it had wrongfully cut his $50,000 annual salary
to $2,000. The case was subsequently settled out of court.

Walsh decided to strike out on his own. His first venture was
Bresea Resources, a junior exploration company that he named after
his sons, Brett and Sean. He tried drilling for oil in Louisiana, but
the petroleum business had nosedived and things went from bad to
worse. The family's only steady income came from Jeannette's
$20,000-a-year job as a legal secretary. The rest depended on luck,
with Walsh gambling heavily on new stock issues.

In 1989 Walsh launched Bre-X. "Bre" derived from Bresea and
"X" stood for exploration. Walsh hunted for gold in Quebec and
joined a diamond rush in the Northwest Territories. His luck was so
terrible that he opened his 1991 annual report with the line, "Yes, we
are still in business."

When he and Jeannette eventually declared bankruptcy, court
records showed they owed $59,500 to fifteen credit card companies
and department stores, including Woolworth's and Canadian Tire. At
age forty-nine, Walsh had nothing to show for his efforts as a stock
promoter but a mortgaged split-level home in the Calgary suburbs
and a 1979 Buick Regal held together by duct tape. He was working
out of his basement, seemingly headed nowhere.

Then his luck changed dramatically. Walsh began an incredible
rise to fortune, helped by John Felderhof, an old geologist buddy
whose main claim to fame was the 1968 codiscovery of a large cop-
per and gold mine in Papua, New Guinea. After gambling his firm's
last $10,000 on a do-or-die trip to Indonesia, Walsh returned to
Calgary with dollar signs in his eyes. Felderhof had persuaded him to
buy gold exploration rights to a creek at Busang, in the jungles of
Borneo. Within months the world's most fabled gold mine was born.

Walsh became the darling of the penny stock-promoting crowd
in Calgary. He was one of their own and he seemed to have hit
the jackpot. This overweight, chain-smoking barfly whose fond-
ness for alcohol brought out his charm—and occasionally his Irish
petulance—was the toast of Canadian capitalism. With Felderhof

handling the mining side, Walsh raised money and took his penny stock enterprise to dizzying heights. He fought off takeover attempts by gold giants, including Placer Dome and Barrick Gold, which enlisted the support of the Indonesian government.

Busang's reserve estimates seemed to rise as fast as Bre-X stock. It was the mother-lode of picks for investors who bought early. Their shares soared from pennies in 1993 to more than $286 by 1996, making millionaires of many. Walsh was apparently sitting atop the biggest gold strike the world had ever seen. And he was rich. He later told securities regulators that he and Jeannette made $45.7 million selling Bre-X shares on the open market in 1995 and 1996. As company insiders, they were obliged to publicly disclose their trading.

At its height, Bre-X had a stock capitalization of $6 billion, exceeding that of Molson, Chrysler Canada, and Coca-Cola combined. The word out of Borneo was that the Busang find contained 200 million ounces of gold. That would have made it history's richest discovery, containing gold worth $100 billion.

But the whole thing came crashing down in March 1997. It started with a report that Bre-X's chief geologist, Michael de Guzman, had fallen out of a helicopter to his death in the Indonesian jungle. Then came an alarming report from Freeport-McMoRan, the company Walsh had struck a deal with after fending off the advances of Placer Dome and Barrick. Freeport-McMoRan said it couldn't match the Bre-X drilling results with its own work on the Busang site.

The site turned out to contain little or no gold. The remarkable assay results were attributed to tampering of core samples—a process known as salting—by adding gold panned from a nearby river. A mining analyst estimated that it took about $40,000 worth of real gold to salt all 268 drill holes. The Busang geology crew had started rigging the core samples shortly after Bre-X bought the exploration rights, hoping to discourage the company from shutting down the project. Strathcona Mineral Services characterized it as a fraud "without precedent in the history of mining anywhere in the world."

The largest gold find in history became the hoax of the century. In the media reports, Walsh changed from a David who fended off the gold industry Goliaths to a disgraced stock promoter whose mission now was to convince the world he was every inch the dupe he appeared to be. "I am wiser and obviously more cynical," Walsh told reporters. "Four and a half years of hard work, and the pot at the end of the rainbow is a bucket of slop." In a telephone conversation with Felderhof, reported by author Jennifer Wells in her book *Fever: The Dark Mystery of the Bre-X Gold Rush,* Walsh said he felt empty and sick. "They fooled me completely," he said. "This is the scam of the century."

Four books were published about the Bre-X scandal, each with its own take on Walsh's culpability. All concluded that he had been conned but that he should have asked the hard questions before selling his dream to investors.

Walsh resigned as chairman of Bre-X and fled to the Bahamas, where he had bought a seaside villa in December 1995. He died there, of a brain aneurysm, at age fifty-two, leaving behind a clutch of unhappy investors and a messy trail of class-action lawsuits. His doctor said that "aside from the aneurysm, Mr. Walsh was in excellent health." Indeed, and aside from the nakedness, Walsh boasted a set of new clothes that would have been the envy of any emperor.

Allan Stein

Folk singer, filmmaker, and radio announcer

1948–1994

Allan Stein wanted to do many things in life. First, he wanted to be a folk singer, which he did as a nineteen-year-old in Calgary during the 1960s. Then he wanted to make movies, which he couldn't do in Calgary, so he moved to Edmonton. Then he wanted to be a radio announcer. He could have done that in Calgary, but he was already in Edmonton so he stayed.

The Calgary folk scene of the 1960s was a lively affair, headquartered in a fabled downtown coffeehouse called the Depression. Joni Mitchell—Joni Anderson at the time—strummed her ukulele and sang "Sloop John B." Will Millar sang the Irish wenching and drinking songs he would later perform for a wider audience as leader of the Irish Rovers.

Allan Stein played at the Depression in between organizing university student demonstrations and working as a meat cutter in his uncle's packing plant. He put together a trio called Fat Chants and played something he called "left-wing swing." A friend recalls that the trio did a terrific version of Cole Porter's "Love for Sale." They also performed original material, including one of their more popular offerings, a tune Stein titled "Don't Eat Nothin' You Can't Spell."

When the folkies went electric, Stein plugged in his guitar, increased the feedback level on his amplifier, and did respectable imitations of Clapton and Hendrix. But it was time for him to be moving on. He wanted to make his name in the film business.

Stein arrived in Edmonton in 1969. The Beatles broke up, the Stones recorded "Honky Tonky Woman," and Stein became a founding partner in a ragtag collective of fledgling filmmakers known as Filmwest Associates. The group's early work included *Ernest Brown: Pioneer Photographer*, a docudrama offering a photographer's lens-eye view of life in Alberta in the early twentieth century. Stein also made television commercials—including a hygiene promo that showed kids how to brush their teeth—industrial safety films, music videos, and educational films.

During the 1970s and 1980s, Stein worked as director, producer, writer, or editor on such film projects as *The Gunfighters, My American Cousin*—the Sandy Wilson coming-of-age movie—and *Shooting Stars*, the story of the unbeatable Edmonton Grads, a female basketball team that dominated the sport in Canada for twenty-five years and ruled as world champions for seventeen. Stein also filmed *Sylvan Lake Summer*, a beach movie being made during a typical Alberta summer, when a snowstorm interrupted the shoot. A visiting reporter suggested tongue-in-cheek that Stein and his partners were "in serious need of psychiatric counselling."

When Stein finished his films, he put on his hat as president of AMPIA, the Alberta Motion Picture Industry Association, and urged movie houses to show them. He wasn't making films for the closet, he said—he wanted his films to be seen. At the time of his death in July 1994, he was working on a movie about the late Winnipeg-born jazz guitarist Lenny Breau, who died in 1984 at age forty-three. Breau was found dead in the swimming pool of his Los Angeles apartment complex, the victim of an apparent strangling. The case remains unsolved.

In 1990 Stein moved into broadcasting as the host of such CBC Radio programs as *Saturday Side Up*, a regional morning show heard across Alberta, and *Edmonton PM*, the local afternoon drive-home show heard in the provincial capital. It was a natural fit for him. As an outspoken advocate for the film industry, he was rarely short of words. "He couldn't even say his name in under two minutes," quipped a friend. In that respect, Stein was different from other CBC announcers. He had opinions and he expressed them.

Stein maintained his links with his folk-singing past after he moved into radio. He emceed regularly at the Edmonton Folk Music Festival, and he occasionally revived his old group, Fat Chants, to play at clubs and folk festivals around the province.

It took a while before Stein and the CBC got used to one another. The corporation wanted neutral and bland; Stein gave unpredictable and provocative. He drove producers crazy with his habit of departing from the prepared script to talk about whatever happened to be on his mind. On one memorable occasion, he went to cover a legislature opening, looked at a script about government bills to be passed during the current session, then decided to talk about colouring books instead. Colouring books, said Stein, were given to all children who visited the seat of Alberta's provincial government. "At last, government we can understand," he commented. It wasn't exactly the kind of public affairs coverage that CBC audiences were used to, but listeners loved it.

His colleagues also liked it, especially when they were not sitting in the control room looking on helplessly whenever Stein decided to make up his own version of the script. They liked this leftover left-wing hippie who wore Birkenstocks and woollen socks to work and who always ate heartily at cocktail parties because, he said, he was a poor filmmaker who couldn't afford regular meals.

Stein loved radio work because it allowed him to talk to new people every day. Every day, he learned more about people and more about life. The more he learned, the more he had to talk about. That was the way he liked it. He could put a name to every aria he had ever heard on CBC Radio's Saturday afternoon opera program and to every piece of greenery he had ever found in his garden.

His death from cancer at age forty-six came as a shock to all who knew him. It seemed inconceivable that a man so full of life should succumb at such a young age.

"He just loved being alive," said a friend. He loved learning and he loved to talk. Life was an ongoing social studies class for Allan Stein. It was also a fountain of opportunity. In his forty-six years, he managed to do all the things he had ever wanted to do in life, and that's a rare achievement indeed.

Afterword

I could not have written *Building a Province: 60 Alberta Lives* without the information and ideas I found in the following books. To their authors, thank you.

Ken Bolton, Grant H. Kennedy, and James B. Stanton, *The Albertans*; E.A. Corbett, *Henry Marshall Tory: A Biography*; Kenneth Dyba, *Betty Mitchell*; Maida Parlow French, *Kathleen Parlow: A Portrait*; John Frederick Gilpin, *Edmonton, Gateway to the North: An Illustrated History*; James H. Gray, *Boy from Winnipeg*; Renie Gross, *Groundwork: Carl Anderson, Farm Crusader*; George V. Higgins, *Impostors*; Peggy Holmes, *It Could Have Been Worse*; Peggy Holmes, *Never a Dull Moment*; Shelagh S. Jameson, Max Foran, Historical Society of Alberta, Chinook Country Chapter, *Citymakers: Calgarians After the Frontier*; Webster Macdonald, *Memoirs of a Maverick Lawyer: Be Jubilant My Feet*; Grant MacEwan, *And Mighty Women Too: Stories of Notable Western Canadian Women*; Grant MacEwan, *Eye Opener Bob: The Story of Bob Edwards*; Grant MacEwan, *Fifty Mighty Men*; William G. Morrow, *Northern Justice: The Memoirs of Mr. Justice William G. Morrow*; Betty O'Hanlon, *Finding a Familiar Stranger;* Kay Sanderson, *Two Hundred Remarkable Alberta Women*; Donald B. Smith, *Chief Buffalo Child Long Lance: The Glorious Impostor*; Fred Stenson, *The Story of Calgary*.

Index

BY CATEGORY